Peter

KU-714-930

Director of ...

RESEARCH HIGHLIGHTS
IN SOCIAL WORK 17

Child Care: Monitoring Practice

CAT No.   3 0 3

RESEARCH HIGHLIGHTS IN SOCIAL WORK 17

Child Care: Monitoring Practice

Jessica Kingsley Publishers

Editors: Isobel Freeman and Stuart Montgomery
Editorial Consultant: Joyce Lishman
Secretary: Anne Forbes

Editorial Advisory Committee:

Professor G. Rochford	University of Aberdeen
Mr M. Brown	Western Isles Islands Council Social Work Department
Ms J. Lishman	Robert Gordon's Institute of Technology
Mr S. Montgomery	Strathclyde Region Social Work Department
Mr D. Murray	Tayside Social Work Department (SSRG Scotland)
Dr A. Robertson	University of Edinburgh
Dr P. Seed	University of Aberdeen
Mr J. Tibbitt	Social Work Services Group, Scottish Office

University of Aberdeen
Department of Social Work
King's College
Aberdeen

First published in 1988 by Jessica Kingsley Publishers Ltd
13 Brunswick Centre, London WC1N 1AF

© 1988 University of Aberdeen, Department of Social Work

British Library Cataloguing in Publication Data

Child care : monitoring practice. ——
  (Research highlights in social work ; 17).
  1. Social service —— Data processing
  I. Freeman, Isobel   II. Montgomery, Stuart
  361.3'028'5   HV41

  ISBN 1-85302-005-0

Printed and bound in Great Britain by
Biddles Ltd, Guildford and King's Lynn

CONTENTS

Contributors

Isobel Freeman   Senior Research Officer. Graduated from Strathclyde
                      University in 1978. She undertook research into Public
                      Attitudes to Poverty and obtained a PhD from the
                      University of Stirling in 1984. In 1980 she joined Strath-
                      clyde Regional Council and has worked there first as
                      research officer and later as senior research officer. Her
                      work with the Social Work Department has involved her
                      in research into many aspects of practice in all client
                      groups.

Stuart Montgomery   Senior Research Officer. Worked as a social worker in
                      Dundee before undertaking research at Aberdeen and
                      then Dundee universities. He spent five years in the
                      planning and development section of Grampian Social
                      Work Department before moving to Strathclyde. He was
                      joint editor of *New Information Technology in Manage-
                      ment and Practice*, also in the Research Highlights in
                      Social Work series.

John Triseliotis   Director of Social Work Education, University of Edin-
                      burgh. He worked as a teacher and social worker in
                      Cyprus before coming to Britain in 1956 where he trained
                      and worked as a social worker. He has published
                      numerous articles and books, especially in the field of
                      adoption and fostering.

Keith Moore   Principal Research Officer. Joined Strathclyde Regional
                      Council in 1975, working first in the Planning Depart-
                      ment, then in the Chief Executive's Section working
                      mainly on deprivation analysis and the development of
                      needs indicators. He moved to Social Work in 1983 to
                      manage the Department's research team.

Fraser McCluskey   Research Officer. Graduated in psychology and sociology
                      from Stirling University in 1978 before joining Strathclyde
                      Region. Obtained the Diploma in Public Administration
                      in 1983. Although specialising in child care and in
                      demographic analysis, he has published several articles on
                      the impact of changes in social security regulations.

Mary Fegan

District Child Care Officer. Graduated in Social Work from Edinburgh University in 1975 and worked as a social worker in Coatbridge. She then worked for a period as an Assistant Area Reporter before returning to social work as a senior social worker in 1979. She became Child Care Adviser in Renfrew division in 1984 before taking up her present post as District Child Care Officer in 1986 in Hamilton/East Kilbride.

Moira Swanson

Research Officer. Graduated in sociology from Strathclyde University in 1981. She managed the fieldwork of two Chronically Sick and Disabled Persons projects before joining the research team in the Social Work Department. Her interests are broad-ranging. As well as carrying out research in the child care field, she is currently researching the impact of the design and regime of a new home for the elderly on the quality of life of the residents.

Richard Fowles

Senior Resource Worker, Adoption and Fostering. He worked as a trainee in Lanark before successfully completing the social work course at Stirling University. He worked as a social worker in the Motherwell Area Team for three and a half years before moving to his present post.

Mel Cadman

Seconded Lecturer, Jordanhill College of Education. His social work training took place at Stirling and Surrey Universities. He has worked in area teams within Strathclyde Region since 1974, mainly in inner city urban areas. He has recently been seconded to Jordanhill College. His major interests are in social work education and the effective interpretation of child care law in social work practice.

Bernadette Docherty

District Officer, Child Care. Graduated from Glasgow University with a law degree in 1975, and went on to take the Diploma in Social Work in 1977. She worked as a generic social worker in Strathclyde and then Central Region before taking up a specialist child care post in Central Region. She returned to Strathclyde as a senior social worker and was appointed to her present post in 1986.

Colin Findlay

Fieldwork teacher in the Department of Child and Family Psychiatry, Royal Hospital for Sick Children, Glasgow. Graduated in social sciences from Paisley College in 1976 and qualified in social work from Glasgow University in 1977. Worked as a basic grade social worker in an area team in Renfrew and in the Charing Cross Clinic, Glasgow, before moving to his present post in 1981. Currently he is seconded to Glasgow University as a part-time tutor and lecturer in the Department of Social Administration and Social Work. Major area of interest is child abuse.

Gordon Findlay

Assistant District Child Care Officer. A qualified social worker, he has worked in social work for many years, originally with the Children's Department, and has always specialised in the child care field. Before taking up his present post he was adoption and fostering adviser in Argyll/Dumbarton Division. He has participated in and chaired a number of the Department's working parties, including one on private fostering.

Editorial

Isobel Freeman and Stuart Montgomery

This issue of *Research Highlights* differs from the normal pattern. In other volumes the main intention has been to summarise research findings relating to a single general theme, and specialist contributors from a range of organisational backgrounds have presented reviews of relevant topics. With one exception, however, all of the contributors to the present issue work in the same organisation – Strathclyde Region Social Work Department – and all of their material draws upon this shared background.

The aim of the book is to discuss and provide examples of how 'in-house' information systems and research projects can be used to inform child care policy and practice. In spite of the focus on one organisational context we hope to raise issues of both method (research and information) and substance (child care) that are of general interest.

The initial chapter is contributed by John Triseliotis, who sets the volume in a wider context, considering how the work discussed in this volume relates to academic research and commenting on the practice issues raised.

The second chapter describes how a computerised child care information system was set up in Strathclyde, how its findings have influenced the department's child care policy and practice, and how in turn it has developed in response to changes in policy. The increasing use of information systems not only leads to changes in the work of in-house research sections but also has major implications for academic researchers. Even if funding arrangements were to return to more generous levels few external researchers could hope to assemble data-sets of the scale and scope of those now held in many social work and social services departments. Yet serious consideration of collaborative investigations has hardly begun.

In chapter three Fraser McCluskey and Mary Fegan use material from the information system to illustrate recent trends in child care admissions. By contrast with many other parts of the UK, Strathclyde's figures suggest an increasing admission rate. In discussing possible explanations for this a number of practice issues are raised, such as whether taking children into public care is an appropriate response to truancy and whether the frequent use of Place of Safety Orders can be justified. The effect of increasing social deprivation is also considered.

Preventing reception into care is the theme of chapters four and five, both of which are based on attempts to monitor innovatory projects. Moira Swanson reviews the progress of a short-stay refuge for older children, while an initiative involving the strategic use of Section 12 funds is discussed by Richard Fowles. Each project appears to have been successful in keeping families together, though both writers emphasise the difficulties surrounding the evaluation of new projects.

While the Regional Council's policy statements underline the need for prevention, they also insist that definite plans should be formulated for all children who do come into care. An important means of ensuring that plans are made and adhered to is the review process, and an investigation of this process is the starting point for Mel Cadman's discussion in chapter six. Patterns of attendance at and organisation of review meetings are explored, in order to measure the extent to which practice matches stated policy. The development of a new review package is then described. Introduced on a pilot basis in part of the Region, its progress was monitored, and the chapter concludes with a summary of the findings and the lessons they suggested.

Chapter seven takes up current issues in child abuse, discussing an analysis of the routine information at present collected. The need for careful and constant monitoring in this controversial area of work is recognised, as is the training and support required by social workers dealing with those cases.

In chapter eight Isobel Freeman considers the changing role of foster parents in temporary placements. Foster homes are seen as the preferred placements for a growing proportion of children received into care, and foster parents today are called upon to carry out a wider range of functions than in the past. Yet the demands which they face are not always sufficiently appreciated by social work professionals. The chapter draws upon data collected by the information system, and upon the findings of a more detailed investigation, in order to show the difficulties that can occur.

Chapter nine focusses on the adoption of babies and young infants. Stuart Montgomery and Gordon Findlay discuss the wider implications of a survey of prospective adopters in Strathclyde, and point to differing models of practice underlying local variations in selection procedures. These differences colour practice with 'special needs' children as well as with babies, leading the authors to conclude that adoption practice in relation to all groups of children needs constantly to be reviewed.

In assembling these contributions we have tried to meet several editorial objectives, and it may be as well to set these out.

We have tried to avoid parochialism, but have sought to present local material in a way that attracts a wider interest and addresses general issues. Indeed we see in this volume a convergence of the themes of earlier editions of *Research Highlights* covering child care, evaluation and new technology. Nevertheless, we admit to thinking that the sheer size of Strathclyde Region, encompassing half the population of Scotland, may of itself give a wider relevance to the local patterns, and we have therefore included some descriptive material.

We have not attempted to cover all areas of social work with children, but have dealt only with those aspects which our information resources could address. In particular we would have liked to consider home supervision and community assessment, but the development of information systems relating to these areas is still in its early stages.

Although we have aimed at a broadly consistent approach, we have not insisted on an identity of opinion. Indeed some of our contributors offer different interpretations of the same findings. And there are differences in political philosophies, which surface, for example, in discussing the relationship between rates of reception into care and indicators of deprivation. In trying to keep to the middle ground, and to avoid the dangers of propaganda on the one hand and expose on the other, we have nevertheless been anxious to avoid blandness, and we see merit in presenting a range of viewpoints. We want to emphasise, however, that the views expressed throughout the book may not necessarily coincide with the official policy of Strathclyde Regional Council.

We want to thank Joyce Lishman, Mike King and John Triseliotis for their valuable editorial suggestions. The editorial advisory group of *Research Highlights* trusted us not to highjack the volume for localised trumpet-blowing, and for this too we are grateful. A number of people within our own department have been supportive: we are particularly grateful to Peter Bates (now of Tayside Region) and Sandy Jamieson in this respect. And we want also to thank the social workers and the clerical and administrative staff without whose cooperation in the recording of everyday work neither this book nor the information systems and research projects on which it is based would be possible.

Having ready access both to our contributors and to two word-processors, we have perhaps indulged in a greater than usual number of redrafts. To Liz Webber in

Glasgow, and Anne Forbes in Aberdeen, we extend our apologies and our warmest thanks.

An Overview of the Studies

John Triseliotis

One of the benefits of the reorganisation of the social work services in the 1970s was the creation of Departments big enough to support research either by appointing staff to carry out in-house research or by contracting it from outside. The papers included in this volume represent part of one Department's (Strathclyde) in-house research contribution in the area of Child Care. Without such opportunities we would have been deprived of these and other small-scale studies which make their own contribution to the development and/or testing of ideas in very specific areas of social work policy, planning and practice. It is unlikely that this gap would have been filled through centrally-funded research. Though we may be a long way behind the Tavistock ideal of 'no research without therapy' and 'no therapy without research', nevertheless we are witnessing modest beginnings from different Social Work Departments, including the non-statutory sector. Unlike big industrial concerns which can explain the spending of money on research in terms of profit and loss, care agencies cannot demonstrate to funding bodies the benefits of research in such 'concrete' terms. There should also be no illusions that knowledge developed through such efforts can do no more than address small scale specific needs and problems [1].

The studies presented here are modest and pragmatic in their scope and are not pursuing large-scale objectives or the building of significant new theory. Like action research, in-house research claims to be relevant to the work of the agency and to bring about changes in its policies, planning and practices where indicated by the findings. The purpose is to produce something that can be of value and of immediate use to the agency rather than simply analyse and 'illuminate'.

There is no difficulty in summing up arguments for and against such studies, but for me the benefit and advantages far outweigh the drawbacks. For a start, they can address issues of immediate concern to policy makers, planners and practitioners looking for some direction in their policy formulations or searching for solutions to problems. Because many of these concerns can be specific to the agency, bigger studies may never pick them up, or by the time they do so, it is usually too late. For the same reasons, in-house research can be much more quickly disseminated and is likely to be more acceptable and more quickly implemented compared to more general research. Furthermore, researchers engaged in in-house studies are under greater pressure to explain and interpret the application potential of their findings to their own colleagues within the organisation. Outside researchers, unless specially contracted, are under no similar obligation, especially those whose main purpose is simply the pursuit of theory rather than its application.

A major criticism that could be levelled at in-house research carried out by the agency's research teams is the obvious one that it is part of the system it is studying and not objective enough, or is not in a position to be over-critical of the 'hand that feeds it', or that it can never be a platform from which the researchers can present 'a critic of the social order'. There is also the view that the researchers' continued interaction with all levels of the organisation's needs and the wish for its survival could influence the results. This argument assumes that outside research can be value-free or ideologically neutral and that preferences do not unintentionally influence the results. In this respect Berridge [2] points out that

> 'all social research emphasises particular value positions and theoretical viewpoints rather than others, whether or not these perspectives are made explicit.'

In the case of action research with which in-house research shares a number of similarities, Rapaport's [1] suggestion for overcoming this problem is the strict adherence to the ethics of research. It could also be said that no generalisations can be made from in-house research because it refers to the policies and practices of a single agency. Yet it would be surprising if the studies outlined here did not raise similar questions about the practices of other agencies. In the end it is up to other agencies to demonstrate whether the findings are true of them or not.

Because of the multiplicity of activities in which social work departments are involved, and the wide range of programmes requiring study, research methods for monitoring or evaluating programmes have to be pluralistic rather than adhere to a single pre-conceived paradigm. The latter is a luxury that can least be enjoyed in in-house research where the researcher's aim is not to refine techniques, though this can be a by-product arising from the activity. For example, the contributors here demonstrate the place of both quantitative and qualitative approaches built into their research designs, including some participant observation in one of the studies described.

Much has been written about the interplay between research and the process of social policy formulation, and particularly the absence of such a relationship.

Robertson and Gandy [3] discern little connection between research findings and subsequent policy development and go on to add that

> 'despite this investment in research, and the generally greater technical sophistication of researchers themselves, it has to be acknowledged that the impact of research on both policy decisions and practice has at best been disappointing.'

Rapaport's [1] edited volume adds to this gloom by chronicling the rise and fall of 'action research' and the disappointments and failures arising from attempts at closer collaboration between researchers, policy makers and practitioners. As an example some of the contributors make reference to the 'negligible' impact of the Community Development Projects on subsequent policy and practice. The fact that the 'short, sharp, shock' treatment is being continued, though the evidence is that it does not work, is another example that political considerations can be more important for continuing or closing a programme or a service irrespective of what research is saying.

The reason, in my view, why many studies had little or no impact on particularly wider social policy, is that the research objectives were too global, and the expectations too ambitious. Influencing social policies at the national level where the stakes are high, is very different from influencing policy at the local level. In the former case, where bigger political and economic considerations are at issue, research is but one of the many variables thrown into the arena of social policy formulation. Smith [4], acknowledging the failure of what he calls 'experimental social administration' on social policy, reluctantly accepts that most decisions are 'solely the product of competing interest groups.' He goes on to argue that research, sometimes, simply serves to heighten the problems of choice between competing groups. The answer to Smith's rhetorical question whether anything can be salvaged, is in less ambitious and more specific studies. Such studies carried out in-house or through contracting-in, can have their impact both at the national and local levels as illustrated by the recognition accorded in the White Paper [5] whose content has evidently been significantly influenced by the recent child care studies summarised in the DHSS report, *Social Work Decisions in Child Care* [6].

An example of the impact of in-house research described here was Strathclyde's change of policy concerning upper age-limits set for would-be adopters. Decision-making within the smaller world of organisations, compared to big government, can be more decisive when backed-up by well-executed research. With one exception, the studies described here had limited objectives in mind such as monitoring specific activities or evaluating outcomes.

Monitoring and Outcome Studies

There are no neat categories under which to classify different types of research carried out in social work departments but Epstein and Tripodis' [7] categories, in an adapted form, can meet most of the requirements. The classification offered is based on three tiers, one following from the other. First, there is research for obtaining basic information to aid policy formulation and the planning of a specific service or programme; the second step is to monitor the operation of the programme; and the final step is its evaluation, or as I would prefer to call it, studying outcomes. The advantage of such an approach is that it helps to establish needs, specify objectives and identify service delivery methods which can then be evaluated. The truth is that such a logical move is not always possible because many services are already there, though this does not mean that a more planned approach cannot be developed. Others have highlighted the dangers of means determining goals where the latter have not been specified from the start.

To plan a new service, e.g. for AIDS sufferers, or to respond to the needs of parents with handicapped children, research can help provide information about the extent of the new need to be met, the population to be reached, the physical and human resources required for the new service from within and outside the agency concerned, and the kind of service delivery methods that have been found to work elsewhere or in similar projects. Using the information planners can specify service goals, identify the users, recruit staff and outline specifications to be followed for the operation of the service.

This sets the scene for the next stage of the research, i.e. the monitoring which starts either at the same time as the new service or subsequently. Most of the studies presented here are of this type (monitoring) though three of them combine monitoring with some outcomes evaluation. According to Epstein and Tripodis [7], programme or service monitoring tells the administration and planners how well a programme is implemented or the extent to which service givers and service administrators follow the specifications set out at the start and whether the service reaches those identified as potential users. Fruin [8] in an article on monitoring in social work agencies defines it as 'a continuing interactive process of systematic surveillance' and argues that to be a continuing process monitoring needs to be an integral part of the agency's system of operation. Goldberg [9] urges the use of monitoring as 'a bottom-up' exercise relating clients' problems to social service input and to its aims and outcomes rather than acting as a mere checking device. She goes on to argue that

> 'if it (monitoring) feeds back the data provided by the service given in a

comprehensible way, then it can enhance the autonomy of practitioners and can contribute to the flexibility and openness of the service system.'

Without being a mere checking device, monitoring can also exercise some quality control, something that can be lost sight of within the general policy and planning procedures.

Any research design that aims to monitor a service has to identify a series of performance standards that are in line with the objectives specified at the outset by the planners. Additional performance standards can usually be obtained from the literature and other research. The studies described here suffer somewhat because of the absence of detailed aims and goals identified at the start of each service, but the researchers utilise general policy statements and guidelines to make up for this.

Three of the studies, i.e. on reviews, the selection of adoptive parents and the analysis of children received into care, offer the opportunity to study decision-making across the agency and identify whether common standards of service delivery exist or not. Not surprisingly, perhaps, the studies reveal a number of inconsistencies some of which point to the need for greater clarity by management and others to practice changes. For example, there are the inconsistencies revealed within divisions in the selection of adoptive parents, including significant differences in the numbers approved or rejected by each division. This ranged from 99 per cent approved by division 'B' in contrast to division 'D' which approved only 78 per cent. The team that rejected most applicants also placed fewer older children. The question to be asked is how far such wide variability within the agency reflects an accurate assessment of need or is a product of the processes and assumptions operated by each division in spite of the general guidelines. The latter possibility seems more likely because differences were maintained even when divisions with similar population structures were contrasted. A legitimate question to be asked is how far some divisions' notions as to 'who can adopt' reflect recent thinking and research or not.

Ideas about the selection and assessment of adoptive and foster parents have shifted significantly over the last ten or so years from being predominantly investigative in nature, moving towards social education, preparation and support, using a combination of group and individual methods [10]. One of the more interesting findings of the study presented here is that contrary to previously held views, something like 36 per cent of women and 45 per cent of men previously approved as adoptive parents were aged 35 and over. Not surprisingly, perhaps, the agency had to reconsider its policy concerning upper age limits.

The analysis provided of children received into care in Strathclyde over a period of time again demonstrates variability between districts and it is, as the study acknowledges, difficult to say whether it reflects an accurate assessment of need or differences in decision-making or in the availability of resources. On the premise postulated by the recent DHSS studies [6] and the White Paper, 'The Law on Child Care and Family Services [5], the prevention of family breakdowns seems more important than the prevention of reception into care. On this principle, an increase in the number received into care say in any one year, may not be a bad thing, unless the children stay in care for too long. Even if we were agreed about the meaning of prevention in operational terms, it is still notoriously difficult to interpret general statistics in such terms. The notion of planned activity in this area is also open to some questioning in view of the study's evidence about the lack of a range of resources and the lack of planning on behalf of many children entering care. In this respect this study raises questions about the use of Section 12 initiatives (which also features in this volume) whose aim was to keep families together. Early exit from care also seems to rely, according to a range of studies, on well prepared admissions and intensive activity towards restoration at least over the first few months following admissions, qualities that were found to be rather lacking here. Similarly, unplanned admissions, as an issue, featured also in the DHSS studies as well as the increase in the number of Place of Safety Orders, including the increase in the number of young people entering care because of relationship difficulties with their parents. As the department seemed to have made little use of fostering for this group of older children, it could point to significant regional variations concerning the type of care received by young people entering care.

The need for a clear child care strategy which starts with prevention of family breakdowns, moving on to restoration of children to their families and then to permanency outwith the natural family, is also supported by the study on child care reviews. This study raises legitimate questions about the nature of reviews and how effective they are in their present form as an instrument of evaluating the accuracy of decision making and of planning, or of controlling the quality of practice. Theoretically reviews should be a time for scrutiny and for every party to be accountable for their part in the overall management of a case. Contractual obligations entered into by social workers, parents or foster parents could be monitored in an atmosphere of shared responsibility. The study raises valid questions not only as to who should be present at reviews but more important, how reviews are prepared and information shared with the participants.

One is reminded of Fisher's [11] and his colleagues' observations concerning the sharing of responsibility with parents and how reviews can be one of the areas to demonstrate such a commitment. Some would also advocate the inclusion at reviews not only of older children, residential staff and foster parents, but also of lay people. This would avoid the danger of internal reviews being too narrowly focussed on internal processes and regulations. It could also help minimise the possibility of social workers developing an opinion about a family which may come to colour all subsequent dealings. Though the Children's Hearing Reviews in Scotland are of a somewhat different nature, nevertheless they have demonstrated that lay people can bring an alternative view to the discussion. Whether such an approach will help parents to feel that they can be better heard and participate more, is too early to say. If, as is shown by these and other studies, child care need involves the children of the most disadvantaged in the community, then one of the issues is how to empower such people. Participation at reviews and sharing the responsibility for what happens to their children is a small start among many others.

Three of the studies presented here could be said to be concerned with outcomes as their ultimate objective, though monitoring features largely in all three. Isobel Freeman's study on the changing role of foster parents inevitably has to look at how placements end. Moira Swanson attempts to assess the impact of an experimental service for teenagers, and finally Richard Fowles examines the implementation and outcome of a preventive strategy through the use of Section 12 initiatives.

As others have pointed out, outcome studies which attempt to assess the value of an activity present complex methodological problems. A major difficulty is agreeing on criteria of 'success' and 'failure' and identifying or developing tools that can measure them. Who sets outcome criteria is also another variable. Each and every one of these agents may have their own views about outcomes. Is this done, for example, by professionals, the clients or the community? In the Fisher et al. [11] study the children's parents had different views from the professionals on how children should be treated while in care, and presumably different notions about what is a 'successful' outcome. There are equally issues about baselines before the start of a service and the absence, not unusual in studies involving people, of a contrast sample. As mentioned earlier, both monitoring, but particularly 'outcome' research, are handicapped if the aims, objectives and expectations from an activity have not been made clear from the beginning. In this respect, the setting of retrospective expectations frequently elicited by researchers are of little value in learning about what has been achieved and how. As Whitaker [12] also reminds us, there is usually no neat package of outcomes: 'Rather', she writes, 'than talking in terms of "success" it is better and nearer to the realities to think in terms of a pattern of gains and losses or costs and benefits.'

Leaving aside some of the reservations made, all three studies provide very useful insights about outcomes which are worth noting. This is especially the case with the study in temporary foster care which is one of the very few available. As temporary fostering goes, the study does not cover 'specialist' fostering because of the stage at which agency practice was at the time the research started. I have also made the point elsewhere [13] that motivation to foster differs with each type of fostering and similarly roles, expectations and outcomes are not always the same. We are only gradually moving towards greater distinctiveness between different types of fostering and this accounts for the fact that findings from one type of fostering do not always relate to those from others [14,15,16]. In other words, contrasting different foster care studies is not always the same as contrasting like with like. Freeman's study has to be seen, therefore, as making a contribution to a hitherto largely uncharted area rather than as failing to confirm, in all respects, processes and outcomes identified by other recent studies.

In spite of what has been said, many of the observations about the process of practice corroborate those of others, including such aspects as: the rather inadequate amount of support made available to foster parents; the absence of a planned contractual approach to fostering; and the difficulties in promoting links between parents and children. These are factors identified by other studies as contributing to greater stability and more favourable outcomes in fostering arrangements. The problems surrounding the maintenance of links between parents and children are not very different from those identified by the DHSS studies [6]. They ranged from foster parents' mixed feelings about access, to transport difficulties and to the absence of social work planning and encouragement. Yet both American and British studies in the last 15 years have been saying that the single factor which is most strongly associated with a child's return home, is parental visiting. The study also makes the pertinent point that 'where reviews were held in the foster parents' home the natural family were less likely to attend....' This illustrates how much we still have to learn about the actual interaction between foster parents and parents. Finally, the more encouraging lower rate of breakdowns, especially compared to studies in the 1960s and early 1970s, may be a feature of either improved practices or due to the type of fostering studied, or both.

The 'Refuge' project which aims to prevent the reception of older children into care was innovative as an integrative resource unit, combining some of the features of a hostel, a drop-in centre and a counselling service. The monitoring part of the study could be helpful to those wishing to set up a similar resource in their area. In this respect the value of the study would have been enhanced further by providing more detail about the way the 'Refuge' linked with other services and how the staff worked with the parents and the children. The latter is of particular importance as most of the children who were referred themselves were still living with their parents at the end of the first year of the scheme's operation. The main question to be asked is what made this possible, including the part played by parents, social workers, children and other services. We are also told that some of the youngsters were set up in supported lodgings and others in bed and breakfast accommodation. Irrespective of our view concerning the concept of prevention of reception into care, there is no doubt that some parents and some children find it a relief to be away from each other for a period. The efforts of the 'Refuge' by providing for this kind of respite without actual reception into care possibly helped also to avoid what sadly has become a stigmatised process. Again, assessing the outcome on behalf of these youngsters proved complex and far from neat. Setting themselves up separately from their families can be the desired goal for some but should it also be measured in terms of durability and 'well-being'? We know from Stein and Carey's [17] study how hard and difficult it is for young people leaving care to live and manage independently in the community even with support from the social services. It is perhaps too much to expect of 16 and 17 year olds, and we still do not know what makes the difference between those who succeed and the rest. Some of the young people were certain that they wanted to have nothing to do with their families again, which presents the social work services with the challenge to devise, in collaboration with voluntary and other services, ways of supporting young people on a long-term basis.

The impact of the Section 12 Initiative, as the author rightly admits, is difficult again to assess because of the absence of a contrast group. The study illustrates the need to develop standardised questionnaires or scales that can measure social and family functioning to help also establish the 'before and after' of the situations. As it was, the study relied as far as outcomes were concerned on the views of the practitioners. The financial and practical needs of the 17 families studied were not the sole problem but were accompanied or complicated by personal and relationship difficulties which could have resulted or been the cause of the practical difficulties. Overall only an insignificant number of children from these families eventually came into care. It also showed that the boundary line between preventing family breakdown and preventing reception into care is rather blurred. The observations about gains made, confirm other studies suggesting that in such situations dealing at least with some of the practical needs of the families early on, helps to demonstrate tangible concern by relieving external stress before beginning to deal with the more personal and inter-personal issues. Within the study it would have been useful to demonstrate how far the initiative described here is part of a wider coherent and consistent policy about prevention and services to families, which includes a range of supportive services at the individual and group level, covering counselling, day care and child-minding, respite services, self-help groups, activity and skills groups, and so on. This is said to highlight the need for a child care theory that encompasses prevention, admission into care, restoration and finally perman- ence outwith the original family. At the moment our thinking and activities are too much constrained by fragmented legislation and isolated concepts about planning and practice.

In conclusion, it is to be hoped that this volume of policy and practice-related studies will become an encouragement for many more similar initiatives to respond to the Seebohm report's challenge that 'social planning is an illusion without adequate facts; and the adequacy of services mere speculation without evaluation' (para. 473).

References

1. Rapaport, R.N. 'Children, Youth and Families'. In Rapaport, R.N. (Ed.) *The Action Research Relationship*. Cambridge, 1985.

2. Berridge, D. *Children's Homes*. Blackwell, 1985.

3. Robertson, A. & Gandy, J. 'Policy, Practice and Research: An Overview'. In Gandy, J., Robertson, A. & Sinclair, S. (Eds.) *Improving Social Intervention*. Croom Helm, 1983.

4. Smith, G. 1985. Referred to in Gandy et al. op. cit.

5. DHSS. *The Law on Child Care and Family Services*. HMSO, 1987.

6. DHSS. *Social Work Decisions in Child Care*. HMSO, 1985.

7. Epstein, I. & Tripodis, T. *Research Techniques for Programme Planning, Monitoring and Evaluation*. Columbia University Press, 1977.

8. Fruin, D. 'The Contribution of Research' *Adoption and Fostering*. 96, 1979, 30-37.

9. Goldberg, M.E. 'Monitoring in the Social Services'. In Goldberg, E.M. & Connelly, N. (Eds.) *Evaluative Research in Social Work*. Heinemann, 1981.

10. Triseliotis, J. (Ed.) *Groupwork in Adoption and Foster Care*. Batsford, 1986.

11. Fisher, M., March, P. Philips, D. & Sainsbury, E. *In and Out of Care*. Batsford, 1986.

12. Whittaker, D. *The Experience of Residential Care from the Perspective of Children, Parents and Care Givers*. Final report to the ERSC, 1984.

13. Triseliotis, J. 'Beckford: Principles of Foster Care and the Practice of Social Work' *Foster Care*. 1986, 12-14.

14. Triseliotis, J. 'Growing up in Foster Care and After'. In Triseliotis, J. (Ed.) *New Developments in Adoption and Foster Care*. Routledge and Kegan Paul, 1980.

15. Rowe, J., Cain, H., Hundleby, M. & Kean, A. *Long-Term Foster Care*. Batsford, 1984.

16. Berridge, D. & Cleaver, H. *A Study of Fostering Breakdowns* Dartington Social Research Unit, 1986.

17. Stein, M. & Carey, K. *Leaving Care*. Blackwell, 1986.

Information Systems and their Implications for Childcare Policy and Research

Isobel Freeman, Stuart Montgomery and Keith Moore

INTRODUCTION

During recent years many social service agencies in the United Kingdom, as elsewhere, have been developing or purchasing computerised information systems. The literature on this topic is now quite extensive, and a number of reviews are available [1,2,3,4]. Although such systems are spreading into most areas of practice, their most common application is in the field of child care. In a study carried out in Great Britain in 1984, Cordingley and her colleagues found that of the 120 authorities responding to their postal survey, 83 had systems relating specifically to child care [5,6].

The present volume of *Research Highlights* can be seen as a case study of such developments. This introductory chapter begins by describing the establishment and refinement of an information system in one social work department – Strathclyde Regional Council, and goes on to show the ways in which routinely-held information is used to monitor, and indeed to shape, policy and practice, and can both stimulate and support more traditional research projects. In doing so it not only discusses substantive child care issues but also points to changes in the nature of research and information work within social services and social work departments, and to changes in the relationship between 'in-house' and 'academic' research.

THE DEVELOPMENT OF THE CHILD CARE INFORMATION SYSTEM

Before 1979 even very basic information on child care practice in Strathclyde was not available. The sex, age and family circumstances of children in care were not known, and there were no reliable statistics on the *number* of children coming into care. These shortcomings were highlighted during 1978, in the course of an officer-member group enquiry into child care policy and practice [7], and in the following year a survey was undertaken of the personal, social and environmental factors associated with admission to care. Information from all reception into care forms completed over a thirteen month period was coded, put onto the computer and analysed. However, although this exercise provided for the first time the detailed material required for planning purposes, there were a number of problems with it. Because the collection of the forms was not a routine feature of everyday administration it was not easy to ensure all were returned, and it is likely that the number of admissions was underestimated. Furthermore, the forms were often only partly completed. For example, rather than a full reason for reception into care being recorded, only the legislation under which the child was admitted would be noted. Incomplete though this information was, it did nevertheless provide a broad picture of the ages of children, the type of placement used, the areas the children came from and their family background [8].

The findings raised a number of issues affecting departmental policy and practice. For example, at a policy level they demonstrated that there was an association between deprivation and reception into care, and were therefore seen by the Council as confirming the relevance of its emphasis on the need for positive discrimination [9]. At a practice level the identification of variations between districts made it possible for clear targets to be set for the districts to work towards.

Due to the widespread recognition of the value of this kind of information it was decided to monitor admissions on a regular basis. Following extensive consultation with practitioners, a new form was devised covering a comprehensive range of items and using, where possible, a tick box approach. This not only ensured standardised data, but also made both the completion of the form and the subsequent coding easier. These are important considerations: as du Feu found from his comparative study of the introduction of computerised systems in two English social services departments, poor form design leads to poor form completion and can adversely colour social workers' wider attitudes to computers [10].

Information on reception into care provided only part of the picture. The need to monitor moves between placements, changes in the legislation under which children were retained in care, and discharges, was quickly realised and work towards the computerisation of transfer and discharge records was begun. Admission, transfer and discharge data, as well as being important in their own right, also provided the basis for a current and historical register of children in care, which made it possible to provide 'snap-shots' at specified points in time, and also to analyse admissions, transfers and discharges not only as care episodes but also cumulatively, as care histories.

The next stage was the setting up of two sub-systems looking at specific aspects of child care: child abuse and parental rights resolutions. The information required was readily available in manual registers, case conference minutes, and committee reports, and the development of data sets from this base was relatively straightforward.

The major intention of these early developments was to provide material to assist practice monitoring and policy planning, with Headquarters staff the main target audience and the main source of suggestions for further refinements. We will come presently to later moves to use the information system to influence practice in more direct ways, but it is useful first to set out the policy context within Strathclyde, and to show the interrelatedness of policy and information.

RELATIONSHIP BETWEEN INFORMATION AND POLICY

The basis of Strathclyde's child care policy can be summarised in five statements referring to six broad strategies. The adoption and continued acceptance of the relevance of the strategies was and is considered in the light of analysis available from the information system, as the paragraphs below illustrate.

1) To provide support for children and families which will enable them to stay in the community (family support service strategy and youth strategy).

The information system has played an important part in the development of preventive services, showing where resources are required, where local prevention strategies are working, and where preventive practice needs improved. For example, it allows us to see whether areas with higher levels of pre-five provision have lower rates of reception into care of pre-fives, and whether areas with good Intermediate Treatment provision have fewer children admitted to List 'D' schools. These findings have been used in arguments for more resources and in consideration of resource deployment. The effects of locally developed preventive strategies, such as single parent support groups, have also been monitored.

2) To ensure children who require to be received into care receive the support they and their families need to enable them to return home (rehabilitation strategy).

Information on those in care, particularly their family characteristics, has implications for rehabilitation. For example, both our own data and other research [11,12] have shown that the families of children in care seldom include both natural parents, and are often subject to changing membership. It is therefore important that policies encourage social workers to be flexible in plans for rehabilitation; for instance, when considering access arrangements it is appropriate to maintain contact with family members other than the natural mother, and the possibility that the child may be rehabilitated with them should be considered. Regular monitoring of the extent to which contact has been maintained shows room for improvement in practice.

Data on the length of time children have been in care are essential if rehabilitative practice is to be monitored. The length of time children require to be in care is related to the reason for their coming into care, their age and the legislation to which they are subject. The relatively detailed information within Strathclyde allows us to look at specific categories of children, and to consider the impact of the route by which they come into care upon their length of stay.

3) To enable children in care to experience family life (home finding strategy).

4) To ensure that those who require residential care while working towards rehabilitation or preparation for independent living is underway receive care of the highest quality (residential care strategy).

Information on both age and reasons for admission is important when considering the home-finding and residential care strategies. Strathclyde, like other authorities, has for several years promoted foster care, but despite this emphasis and despite an increase in the proportion of children placed into foster care, there has been no absolute increase in the number of children fostered. Similarly, the proportion of older children fostered, although increasing, remains relatively small. Our data allow the effect of both the general stress laid upon fostering and the development of specific schemes to find fostering resources for children in 'harder to place' categories to be monitored. The data also allow the way in which the residential sector is being used, and the practice of developing homes with particular expertise in specific tasks such as preparation for permanent foster care or rehabilitation, to be monitored.

5) To recognise the right of children leaving care to receive continued support (supported accommodation strategy).

Finally, admission and discharge data show that support and preparation for independent living are required not solely by children with a long care history but also by those who have only recently come to the attention of the department and whose problems at home or at school started in adolescence. It is clear that our strategies for dealing with these groups must take into account not only the similarities but also the differences in the problems they experience. As can be seen in Moira Swanson's chapter, information on background characteristics, problems and care experiences can be used to develop appropriate strategies for providing support to older children.

FUTURE SYSTEM DEVELOPMENT – FROM SOCIAL SURVEY TO OFFICE AUTOMATION?

We have always acknowledged that if information which is largely supplied by social workers is to be accurate, the system must benefit them and they must recognise its value. One of the ways in which we try to demonstrate to teams the importance of this information is by ensuring feedback is available to them, and not only to senior management, at regular intervals. All social service agencies operating computerised systems are faced with this issue; an interesting account of an attempt to devise partly-automated feedback arrangements for social workers participating in a community care scheme for elderly people in an English authority is given by Challis and Chesterman [13].

In addition to providing statistical feedback we have encouraged social workers and managers to use system outputs in planning and monitoring their practice. Examples of this would include; using the system, in some teams, as a prompt for forthcoming reviews of children in care: monitoring repeat admissions of particular children; monitoring admissions and placements of very young children; identifying children in their mid-teens, to ensure that adequate planning for leaving care takes place.

In spite of these developments the system shows many signs of its origins in a one-off social survey, and can be regarded as a constellation of partly-linked 'institutionalised social surveys.' That is to say, the major emphasis to date has been placed on statistical output rather than on day-to-day operational and administrative requirements. Forms are still batched centrally before input to the computer is carried out, and although the recent restructuring of the department has shortened lines of communication in this as in other respects, the delays and inaccuracies inherent in batch-processing persist [14]. Most analysis, similarly, is based on the Statistical Package for the Social Sciences which was developed to meet the needs of survey researchers rather than to satisfy operational requirements within social services [15], although we complement this with more flexible routines which were written in-house.

Future plans, however, include not only the extension of the system's scope (to embrace, for example, all child care reviews, and child abuse referrals as well as registrations), but also envisage better integration with administrative procedures so that, eventually, good quality statistical information will be provided simply as a by-product of ordinary record-keeping.

Other departments have taken different approaches to system design and development, but the one we have followed is quite commonplace and has been described by Cordingley, in her survey report, as a 'modular' strategy:

'Modular developments were designed so that standards, definitions and formats used in one module of the system would not be incompatible with future developments. There often, though not always, was an overall strategic plan from the outset, in spite of what might have appeared as piece-meal development' [6].

She distinguishes this approach from the 'holistic' introduction of comprehensive systems covering all client groups, all services and all resources, on the one hand, and the 'ad hoc' development of unrelated applications on the other.

Cordingley's survey was the second to be undertaken by LAMSAC. If there is to be a third it will make interesting reading, for some exciting developments are already underway. In Strathclyde we have been evaluating the suitability of viewdata (teletext) as a medium for storing procedures relating to child care and to other client groups [16,17]. Examples of work in other parts of the UK include a proposal for a computer-based system for recording child abuse case conferences [18], and 'expert-systems' and 'decision-support systems' aimed at assisting in the diagnosis and treatment of child abuse [19,20].

RELATIONSHIP BETWEEN INFORMATION AND RESEARCH

Regularly collected information provides us with a wealth of data suitable for use in monitoring, as the chapters in this volume on reception into care and child abuse show. There is however a need for additional investigations to be undertaken to illuminate areas not yet covered by the information system. The chapters on prospective adopters and reviews provide examples of such work. Not only did the projects on which they are based satisfy *ad hoc* needs, but they also demonstrated the value of collecting some of the material on a regular basis and helped identify how it could be obtained. They are examples of how yesterday's research project can become today's information system.

More qualitative forms of enquiry will always be required, and are perhaps especially necessary in relation to consumer/client views, the evaluation of methods of work, and social workers' decision-making [21]. The chapters on temporary fostering, on the Section 12 initiative and on preventing reception of older children into care, provide examples of some of the more qualitative investigations undertaken recently within Strathclyde. More of this type of research is required but even here the information system makes a contribution by providing background material and by allowing hypotheses to be more specific.

IMPLICATIONS FOR ACADEMIC RESEARCH

The development of more comprehensive and more sophisticated information systems in the social services offers the academic community two significant research opportunities, for the impact of such systems is a valid and important research *topic* in its own right, and the data which they collect and store constitute a potentially valuable research *resource*. There has not been a rush to grasp these opportunities.

The impact of information systems has received very little empirical study, even although several commentators have pointed to the possibility of significant effects upon the nature of professional supervision and workload management [22], upon the nature of accountability both within departments and in relation to local and national political authority [1,23] and upon the work content and job-satisfaction of clerical and administrative staff [24]. Nor has there been much research interest in the processes by which staff in social service agencies achieve the categorisations of their work that computerised systems demand, or, in other words, how the diversity of a social work case is reduced to one or several of the stark choices offered by an input form. A vast literature, drawing upon the insights of interactionist and ethnomethodological sociology (of which Smith [25] provides a useful review) has grown up around the subject of administrative 'people-processing', but we do not know how computerisation has impinged upon such 'processing' nor, importantly, about the differential impacts of different kinds of system (for example, social survey as against office automation). As Cicourel has observed, research undertaken from such a perspective can bring about improvements to information systems by suggesting ways to control for at least some possible sources of error [26].

Similarly, there have been few examples of collaborative work involving academics in the analysis of in-house data, or even in using such data to select sample cases for detailed investigation. This is not to say that the possibility has been overlooked. Reviewing general trends in child care research for the first volume of *Research Highlights*, Tibbitt concluded that although researchers had made a contribution in a number of areas of policy and practice, 'there remain many more questions than answers', and he proposed changes in both focus and method in order to make research more helpful to service providers. For example, he observed:

> 'Much can ... be gained from the scrutiny of management information and case records held within agencies. Indeed a powerful argument for the improvement of recording procedures is the light such information can throw on the efficacy of particular sorts of practice' [27].

Any attempt to develop a joint approach to the analysis of such data would of course need to take note of the general problems of 'secondary analysis' [28,29]. However, our experiences of joint working, in relation to another of Strathclyde's information systems, demonstrates that such an approach can be worthwhile [30].

References

1. Glastonbury, B. *Computers in Social Work*. MacMillan, London, 1985.

2. Smith, N.J. *Social Welfare and Computers: A General Outline*. Longman Cheshire, Melbourne, 1985.

3. Horobin, G. & Montgomery, S. (Eds.) *New Information Technology in Management and Practice. Research Highlights,* No.13, Kogan Page, London, 1986.

4. Ward, D. 'Client Information Systems in the Social Services'. In England, J.R., Hudson, K.I., Masters, R.J., Powell, K.S. & Shortridge, J.D. (Eds.) *Information Systems for Policy Planning in Local Government*. Longman, London, 1985, 113-125.

5. Cordingley, E.S., Clark, E.E.M. & Rajan, L. *Computerisation in Social Services and Social Work Departments: A National Survey, 1984*. LAMSAC, London, 1984.

6. Cordingley, E. 'Patterns of Computer Use in the UK'. In Horobin, G. & Montgomery, S. (Eds.) *New Information Technology in Management and Practice. Research Highlights*, No.13, Kogan Page, London, 1986.

7. *Room to Grow*. Strathclyde Regional Council, 1979.

8. *Who Are They?* Strathclyde Regional Council, Social Work Department, Glasgow, 1979.

9. *Social Strategy for the Eighties*. Strathclyde Regional Council (no date).

10. Du Feu, D. *Computers and Social Workers: the Reception of a Computerised Client Record System in Social Services Fieldwork District Offices*. Unpublished PhD thesis, University of Edinburgh, 1982.

11. Fisher, M., Marsh, P., Phillips, D. & Sainsbury, E. *In and Out of Care*. Batsford, London, 1986.

12. Millham, S., Bullock, R., Hosie, K. & Haak, M. *Lost in Care*. Gower, Aldershot, 1986.

13. Challis, D. & Chesterman, J. 'Feedback to Front-Line Staff from Computerised Records: Some Problems and Progress' *Computer Applications in Social Work and Allied Professions*. 3, 1987, 12-14.

14. Montgomery, S. 'Implementing and Managing Computerised Client Information Systems'. In Horobin, G. & Montgomery, S. (Eds.) *New Information Technology in Management and Practice. Research Highlights*, No.13, Kogan Page, London, 1986.

15. Nie, N.H., Hull, C.H., Jenkins, G., Steinbrenner, K. & Bent, D.H. *Statistical Package for the Social Sciences*. 2nd edition. McGraw Hill, New York, 1975.

16. McNicol, A. 'Viewdata' *Computer Applications in Social Work and Allied Professions*. 3, 1987, 20.

17. Montgomery, S. 'Soft but not Squidgey: Obtaining Staff Resources through Special Funding Measures' *Computer Applications in Social Work and Allied Professions*. 4, 1987.

18. Sharron, H. 'Can Machines Replace Social Workers?' *New Society*. 21 March 1986, 502-503.

19. Toole, S. 'Solving Old Problems with a New System' *Social Services Insight*. 17 July 1987, 10.

20. Algie, J. 'Weighing up Priorities' *Community Care*. 11 September 1986, 18-20.

21. Pinker, R.A. *Research Priorities in the Personal Social Services*. SSRC, London, 1978.

22. Goldberg, E.M. & Warburton, R.W. *Ends and Means in Social Work*. Allen & Unwin, London, 1979.

23. LaMendola, W. 'Software Development in the USA' *Computer Applications in Social Work and Allied Professions*. 1, 1987, 2-7.

24. Crompton, R. & Jones, G. *White-Collar Proletariat. Deskilling and Gender in Clerical Work*. MacMillan, London, 1984.

25. Smith, G. *Social Need*. Routledge & Kegan Paul, London, 1980.

26. Cicourel, A.V. *The Social Organisation of Juvenile Justice*. Heinemann, London, 1976.

27. Tibbitt, J. 'Further Research Needed'. In Reinach, E. (Ed.) *Decision Making in Child Care*. Research Highlights No. 1, Scottish Academic Press, Edinburgh, 1981.

28. Stacey, M. *Methods of Social Research*. Pergammon, Oxford, 1969.

29. Moser, C.A. & Kalton, G. *Survey Methods in Social Investigation*. Heinemann, London, 1971.

30. Becker, S. & McPherson, S. *Poor Clients*. University of Nottingham, 1986.

Trends in Child Care Admissions

Fraser McCluskey and Mary Fegan

INTRODUCTION

Since 1984 data on between two and three thousand admissions to care per year have been collected and analysed. Detailed data is now available on over 7,000 admissions. This chapter presents this information and discusses some of the issues raised by the analysis.

As the previous chapter stated, Strathclyde Regional Council are committed to a policy of maintaining children within their own families and their own communities whenever this is consistent with their welfare, and since the formation of the Region in 1975 the resources to give effect to this policy, known as 'The Family Support Strategy', have been developing. These include Family Centres, Home Support and Daycare Schemes, and the Section 12 Initiative described by Fowles in this volume.

Despite this, there has been an increase in the number of child care admissions, with 2,675 during the financial year 1985/86, compared to 2,438 in 1984/85[1]. And this is not just a temporary hiccup; in 1981 the Council produced a document entitled *Who Are They?* which showed that between May 1978 and May 1979 (a 13 month period), 2,283 children were received into care [1]. From a historical perspective, therefore, the number of admissions to care has been showing an underlying increase since at least 1978.

That increase assumes greater significance when considered against wider demographic trends. Children aged under 16 fell from 24 per cent of the population in 1981 to 21 per cent in 1985 [2]. As a consequence the rate of admission has risen from 3.4 per 1,000 population aged 0-16 in 1979 to 4.4 per 1,000 in 1986. Other local

---

[1] Footnote: These figures exclude children subject to Children's Hearing Supervision Requirements in terms of Section 44 [1](a) of the Social Work (Scotland) Act 1968 where no condition of residence is attached. It should also be noted that while admissions are increasing the number of children in care at any one point in time is decreasing.

authorities have experienced quite different patterns; many report that in the last few years admissions have either remained static or declined.

There is no easy explanation for Strathclyde's increase. Indeed, the complexity of the situation is clear when one considers that within the Region itself the rate of reception into care varies from 6.4 per 1,000 children in one district to 2.1 per 1,000 in another. Some districts have even shown a decrease in the last few years.

Greater understanding is achieved if the figures are considered against other social, economic and demographic changes taking place within the Region, for it is clear that the level of deprivation has increased significantly within Strathclyde in comparison to other areas. Unemployment in the Region rose from 95,000 in 1979 to 195,000 in August 1986, an increase of 105 per cent. This compares to an increase of 85 per cent for Scotland. Over the same period the number of people relying on Supplementary Benefit as their main income increased by 101 per cent in the Region compared with 83 per cent for Scotland. Moreover, since 1981 there has been a 50 per cent increase in the number of single parent households in the Region, the figure now standing at 28,500.

Since numerous research studies have indicated a strong correlation between poverty and admission to care[4,5,6], it might at first seem unsurprising that as the level of deprivation within the Region has increased so, too, has the admission rate. Yet, as we have seen, some other parts of Scotland have experienced a decline in admission rates, notwithstanding growing poverty. It is our view that the source of our increased admission rate is to be found in a complex interplay of social trends, local policies and a more sophisticated and more accurate recording system. We will try to tease out these issues in a later section, after describing some of the characteristics of the children coming into our care and pointing to some wider policy and practice implications of our findings.

WHO ARE THE CHILDREN BEING RECEIVED INTO CARE?

The reception into care package introduced in 1984 records extensive information about the child, his or her carers, previous periods in care, and living conditions prior to admission. It also covers reason for admission, preferred and actual placements, and proposed placement timescales. These variables enable a range of practice issues to be monitored.

Reasons for Admission

Prior to the introduction of the computerised package, social workers were merely asked to state the statute under which the admission was made. As a result, reasons for admission were never monitored in any systematic way. Since 1984, however, a detailed list of reasons, 35 in all, has been available to the workers completing the forms. The table below presents the most common reasons given for admissions during 1985/86.

TABLE 1

Reasons for admission

	Primary Reason %	Underlying Reason %
Physical illness of female carer	8	5
Mental disorder of female carer	4	3
Lack of parental care	9	8
Truanting	10	5
Child committed offence	8	6
Outwith parental control	14	16
Deteriorating relationship with carers	9	11
Suspected child abuse	3	1
Same household as someone suspected of child abuse	4	3
Carer drunk	5	4
Others (or none*)	26	38

* Underlying reasons only.

In this short chapter we can point to only some of the issues raised by these figures.

The number admitted because of truancy appears to be increasing and the removal of children from home for this reason is a major area of concern. While there is no doubt that for many children truancy is simply a symptom of wider family and relationship problems, for a large number of others dissatisfaction with school is the main reason. To remove such children from their families seems to us to be misguided, not least because of the major difficulties in re-integrating into ordinary schooling children who have experienced residential education [7]. There is an urgent need for the Education and Social Work Departments to liaise closely to help prevent unnecessary removal of children from home. Joint working can achieve a reduction in the numbers of receptions into care for truancy. There is also a need, we suggest, for the members of Children's Panels (who in Scotland have the responsibility of dealing with many truants [8]) to take a more considered view of this problem. Although their obligation to uphold the law may predispose them toward residential disposals, they need to understand that social work alone, or indeed removal from home, will not resolve young people's dissatisfaction with education.

Two other reasons for admission are worthy of comment: 'outwith parental control' and 'deteriorating relationship with carers'. These categories are very similar, and since social workers often have difficulty in choosing between them they can be considered together. More detailed analysis shows that the peak age for admissions for these reasons is in the 12-15 year age band. Many of these young people are admitted to care under Section 15 of the Social Work (Scotland) Act 1968, that is, on a voluntary basis.

This group of young people is probably the most difficult to rehabilitate, and there is clearly a need to develop a better range of preventive resources, as well as ensuring a high level of access following reception into care. An example of such a resource would be the Short Stay Refuge, which is discussed by Swanson in this volume.

Legislative Basis of Admission

The following Table provides a breakdown of the main legislative categories under which children were received into care during 1985/86[2].

TABLE 2

Main legislation

Legislation	%
Section 15 (voluntary care)	45
Section 37 (Place of Safety Order)	22
Section 44 [1](b) (residential supervision)	10
Section 43 [4] (assessment order)	11
Others	12

One of the significant findings of the study of legislative types has been the increasing use of Place of Safety Orders. As a proportion of all admissions, these

[2] Footnote: This refers to the Social Work (Scotland) Act 1968.

have consistently increased over the last four years, culminating in the 1985/86 figures of 22 per cent. As a result, voluntary admissions have dropped from 54 per cent of all admissions in 1983/84 to 45 per cent in 1985/86. The Scottish Office, in their latest statistical bulletin on children in care, have also reported an increase in other Scottish Regions' use of Place of Safety orders, so much so that this category is no longer merely included in the 'other' column of the statute table [3].

Whether this is a short term trend remains to be seen. In Strathclyde, however, a clear picture is emerging of the types of children most likely to be received into care under a Place of Safety Order. These are: children under 12 years of age where child abuse is suspected, or where there is an alleged lack of parental care, and children under 8 years of age where the carers have been found to be drunk. These examples are normally referred to as 'care and protection' cases, where the legislation has been used to protect children from a 'parental act or parental failure'. By contrast, in cases involving the illness of the carer voluntary admission is used much more frequently.

When older children are considered, offences, truancy, being judged to be outwith parental control or to have a deteriorating relationship with carers, are the main factors leading to admission. In these instances Sections 15, 44 (1)(b) and 43 (4) are more frequently used. The following table gives an indication of how age and legislative category are related.

TABLE 3

Relationship between age and legislation

	Voluntary Admissions Section 15 %	Place of Safety* Orders Section 37 %
0–4 years	37	41
5–8	13	21
9–11	11	14
12–15	37	23
16–17	2	1
Total	100	100

* Place of Safety Orders are authorised by sherriffs and allow the compulsory reception into care of a child for a 21 day period.

When legislation type is compared with expected duration in care it emerges that nearly one third of those received under Place of Safety Orders are expected to be in care for more than seven weeks, compared with only one quarter of Section 15 cases (voluntary care). This timescale incorporates the approximate period required for a case to 'go for proof' [9] and then be returned to a Children's Hearing for disposal. Whether all children admitted under Place of Safety Orders require to remain separated from their parents throughout the proof process is, however, open to question, for many are eventually returned home on supervision requirements. This is of particular concern when one considers that the majority of Place of Safety Orders are taken on children under five years old.

The increasing use of emergency compulsory procedures raises a set of wider concerns, for as Packman [10] has observed:

> 'being *compelled* into care carries a high risk that the admission itself will be hasty, ill-prepared and even traumatic ... (and a high risk that) parents lose control over decisions which affect their children's lives, not only at the point of entry, but throughout the time their children remain in care.' (emphasis original)

We shall return to this issue, in discussing the extent to which admissions were said to be planned or unplanned. Another interesting point to emerge from the analysis is the use made of Section 43 (4)(assessment), under which young people can be required to reside in an Assessment Centre for a period of approximately 21 days. In 1985/86 over 300 children in Strathclyde were placed in Assessment Centres under this section. Of these a significant number were subsequently returned to their own homes.

The use of this section is a matter of controversy. There is a widespread view that it can be used inappropriately, not to enable investigation of alternative disposals, but as a punitive measure, to teach youngsters a lesson, or even simply to allow a cooling-off period. To the extent that this is the case it is a cause for concern, for assessment orders carry an implication that the youngsters are prepared to cooperate with the assessment process. If they are not prepared to do so, or if they are considered a risk to themselves or others, then they can be held in assessment centres under warrant.

A further concern is the evidence [11] that residential assessments are likely to produce residential recommendations. For these reasons, Strathclyde Regional Council has taken the view that for a large number of children alternative forms of assessment may be more appropriate. Apart from the issues raised above, a large percentage of children in this category are already known to social work staff. Indeed, social workers describe a high number of these admissions as planned admissions, suggesting that the recommendations had been made by the social workers themselves. For a large number of social workers residential assessment was traditionally the only way of resolving problems with case management. Such help can clearly be offered to many young people while they remain at home, and as a result Strathclyde has made a clear commitment to develop day care and community-based assessment, and is committed to reducing the number of residential placements available. It will clearly take some time before these new resources influence practice both of social work staff and of Children's Panel members, who in effect authorise 43 (4) placements. Through time it will be interesting to note the change in balance between 43 (4) residential assessments and the number of young people being held on warrant within Assessment Centres.

Planned and Unplanned Admissions and Access Plans

Sixty three per cent of all admissions to care in 1985/86 were considered by social workers to be unplanned. The percentage of unplanned admissions has increased over earlier years. Although the precise definition of an 'unplanned' admission is difficult, it clearly implies that reception into care was not part of the social worker's current plan for the child. Consequently these placements are likely to have been arranged at very short notice, and we have to ask whether the nature of the admissions did not itself exacerbate an already difficult situation or lead to further straining of relationships between parents and children, or between parents and social workers.

Some 44 per cent of all unplanned admissions were made on a voluntary basis (Section 15). We have already seen that this section is normally used for young people aged 12 or over who are considered to be either outwith parental control or to have a deteriorating relationship with their carers. Such young people are not considered to require protection from their family. In these circumstances we have to ask why time cannot be taken to plan such admissions. Equally, we are concerned by the number of very young children coming into care under Place of Safety Orders. Some 36 per cent of unplanned admissions invoked this section and since, as noted above, these orders typically apply to the under-fives, this means that many young children entering care do so during a crisis.

The high number of unplanned admissions in Strathclyde is clearly an area for concern, particularly since numerous research works [12] have established that in emergency placements the role and views of the parents are often ignored and many are left feeling aggrieved and embittered. The failure to involve parents in the admission process must have serious consequences for early rehabilitation, particularly when one considers that admission to care is the first step towards rehabilitation.

The setting up of a group whose function is to act as a gatekeeping mechanism in some areas, i.e. to assess planned admissions prior to admission and review unplanned admissions retrospectively, has helped reduce the number of admissions to care, especially the number of unplanned admissions. This approach has also resulted in improvements in the quality of care provided in situations where reception into care was felt to be appropriate, for example, by providing foster placements for a higher proportion of children. This approach is now being extended to the whole of the region.

Another important factor in the rehabilitation process is the level of contact between parents and children at the time of and following reception into care. The importance of access in aiding early successful rehabilitation is well documented. For example, in *Lost in Care* [13] Millham and his colleagues found the maintenance of close family contact to be the single best indicator that a child would leave local authority care rapidly. And there was a wider benefit of close contact:

> 'Children and adolescents, even if their chances of returning home are slim, function better psychologically, socially and educationally if they remain in regular contact with their families.'

In Strathclyde the amount of parental access is initially recorded on the reception into care form. More frequent contact is estimated for children who have planned rather than unplanned admissions (17 per cent of planned admissions, for which details were available, would have no contact, compared with 22 per cent of unplanned ones). The overall figures are, however, worrying. Twenty per cent of carers would have no contact whatsoever while their child was in care. In 19 per cent there was no record of what the level of contact should be, while in over 20 per cent it was expected to be monthly or less frequent. Again, when one considers age and level of contact, major concerns are identified. Only 41 per cent of unplanned admissions for the under-fours recorded either daily or weekly contact.This is of particular concern since in the recently-produced Parental Access guidelines minimum levels of access were identified as three times weekly for children under five if rehabilitation was to be successful.

PLACEMENTS

Like many other authorities, Strathclyde does not yet provide a range of resources which reflect the varying needs of the children who require to come into care. For example, while Strathclyde is committed to a policy of family care, Table 4 shows that only 12 per cent of those aged 12 years or over at admission were placed in foster placements. Young people aged 12 and over make up 50 per cent of all children received into care. While acknowledging that some are more appropriately placed in residential care, a large number clearly are not being placed in preferred placements because of a lack of resources.

TABLE 4

Relationship between age and placement (% within each age-band)

	0–4	5–7	8–11	12–14	15–16	17+
Related fostering	8	7	6	1	1	–
Non-related fostering	73	59	31	7	3	–
L.A. children's home	8	24	50	37	35	66
Assessment centre	–	–	5	42	57	–
Other residential	11	10	9	13	4	33
TOTAL	100	100	100	100	100	100

In order to develop family type placements the Council is encouraging the use of relatives to provide care and prevent actual reception into care. In addition, strategies have been developed to provide more varied fostering resources such as emergency fostering schemes and special fostering placements. Residential care is still seen as necessary in some cases. The Council has recently produced a residential care strategy for the 1980s entitled 'Home or Away' [14], which proposes the development of specialist units within existing resources to meet the needs of young people coming into care. It envisaged, for example, a refuge resource for a period of a few nights for young people experiencing temporary upheaval; short term respite for family crises; longer term treatment programmes linked to preparation for independent living.

Reinach [15] observed a correlation between socio-economic class and placement type, with children of unemployed families being placed in residential settings to a larger extent than those with parents in employment. This 'discrimination' does not appear to feature in Strathclyde. The overriding criterion for placement in residential care is a child's age, although other considerations, such as the number of siblings being received into care, also affect the placement type.

At present social workers are asked to record the recommended as well as the actual placement. The high correlation between recommended and actual placement for residential care suggests that social workers interpret 'recommended' to mean 'available'. In future it would be useful if social workers receiving children into care provided an outline of the types of resources which, had they been available, might have prevented admission. This could allow a further development of a preventive strategy.

POVERTY AND RECEPTION INTO CARE

At the beginning of this chapter reference was made to the increasing levels of deprivation and poverty within Strathclyde, and it was suggested that this has contributed to the increasing numbers of children received into care. This section considers the relationship between poverty and vulnerability to reception into care in more detail.

Are children from poor families more likely to be received into care? Strathclyde uses three fairly well established indicators to denote need and susceptibility to poverty. These are:

[1] Large families, i.e. those with three or more children.

[2] Single parent households, i.e. where only one adult lives in the house.

[3] Families whose main income is state benefit.

TABLE 5

Households of children received into care

Those scoring on all three indicators	26%
Those scoring on any two indicators	54%
Those scoring on only one indicator	17%
Those not scoring on any of the indicators	3%

This Table shows that 80 per cent of all children received into care come from households which scored on two or more of the above indicators. This would suggest that socio-economic factors are playing an even larger part in determining receptions into public care than they did three to four years ago. The Regional Council's report on children received into care in 1981 [1] did not show deprivation to be quite as significant an indicator of reception into care as the above statistics suggest: 75 per cent of admissions at that time scored on two or more of the indicators.

Are all poor children, therefore, susceptible to reception into care?

Poverty alone does not cause reception into care. Many thousands of children of unemployed parents and single parents grow and live normally in communities with minimal social work involvement. It must be acknowledged, however, that additional social, domestic and health burdens are imposed by financial stress, with the consequential threat of family breakdown. Works by Townsend and the Black report on health and inequality help highlight the relationship between poverty and ill health(16,17).

In addition, an analysis of the Regional computerised referral system shows (covering *all* referrals for social work assistance) that families from the lower socio-economic groups tend to make more use of social work services than other groups [18]. Inevitably, social work staff are more likely to come into contact on a regular basis with poor families in deprived housing estates. Their presence and that of other related staff will increase the possibility of detection of neglect and abuse, for example, in such areas. This is not to say, however, that such problems do not exist in other socio-economic groups. There is a view, which while speculative, would suggest that such families tend to pursue the medical as opposed to the welfare model of intervention, where issues of confidentiality often 'protect' families from the welfare model and subsequent public scrutiny. Examples exist within Strathclyde where such 'problem' children from these families are more likely to be admitted to the adolescent hospitals as opposed to formal care systems. As a consequence, reception into care is not formally recorded, although the effect of removal is similar.

Concerns about a simple correlation between poverty and threat of reception into care are highlighted further in the recent report by Fife Regional Council's Reporter's Department [19] which referred to a strong association between families with unemployed parents and referrals to children's hearings. In all child abuse referrals, the children who were taken to a hearing because they were in need of care and protection came from families where the head of the household was unemployed. While this would suggest that child abuse was largely a socio-economic problem, certain forms of child abuse are just as prevalent in more affluent families. Again, such families are considered to be better equipped to maintain their privacy and isolation, concealing their private lives and personal difficulties from the intrusion of social workers.

Finally, there is the view that the perceptions and prejudices of social workers and other professionals contribute to children from poorer families being more vulnerable to reception into care. O'Toole et al. [20] have, for example, argued that the labelling of child abuse amongst the lower socio-economic groups is as much a factor of the 'social distance' between social worker and client as of the extent of the abuse itself. This study showed that where the parent and the professional worker enjoyed a similar socio-economic background and income, parents were less likely to be considered 'abusive' and any injuries were subsequently regarded as accidental. However, where the social distance between the professional worker and the client was great, there was a positive association; poor families and families with low socio-economic status were prone to be labelled 'abusive' with their children's injuries diagnosed as 'non-accidental'. In the same way, cases of lack of parental care', 'neglect', 'young offenders' etc., are more likely to be explained away by affluent families in a way which is not as acceptable from lower socio-economic groups.

The view that poverty alone causes reception into care cannot be sustained. Many other factors influence the delicate balance which exists, including the possible value judgements of involved professionals, including social work personnel, but there is no doubt that poverty can be a contributory factor.

CONCLUSION

This chapter has considered some of the information which has been extracted from the computerised child care information system in Strathclyde with a specific emphasis on reception into care data. The information has highlighted a number of practice trends, some of which give cause for concern, namely:

(a) The increase over time of the numbers of children being received into care, especially when this is against a background of a reducing child population.

(b) The increase in use of Place of Safety Orders, especially among younger children in 'care and protection cases' and the fact that many are anticipated to be in care for seven weeks or more.

(c) The frequent use of residential assessments as first placements.

(d) The frequent use of unplanned admissions with associated poor levels of parental access.

(e) The high number of children received into care from deprived backgrounds.

(f) The lack of foster placements, particularly for children aged 12 or over, who make up over 50 per cent of all those received into care.

(g) The increase in the numbers of young people being received into care because of lack of parental care/outwith parental control.

(h) The lack of a range of resources in general.

Attempts have been made to explain a few of these trends, both in factual and speculative terms. Strathclyde Regional Council has attempted to address some of these issues through the development of a number of approaches. Examples are as follows:

(a) *Social Strategy for the 80s*: The Regional Council has committed itself to a policy of positive discrimination to ensure that scarce resources are provided in the areas of greatest need and highest deprivation.

(b) *District Admissions Support Unit*: All Districts are now required to develop a gatekeeping mechanism to monitor the application of the prevention strategy as it relates to reception into care.

(c) *Community-Based Assessments*: An emphasis is now being placed on the need to develop a range of resources which will allow for the assessment of children in their community. Specialist assessment co-ordinators have been appointed to assist with these developments. The closure of the two Residential Assessment Centres should help encourage this development.

(d) *Youth Strategy*: The Regional Council is now developing a range of resources for young people at risk, with the major focus being on preventative community resources.

(e) *Child Care Reviews*: The present system of child care reviews is being developed to help ensure that appropriate plans are being made for children received into care, and that decisions are monitored. Additionally, the use of written contracts is also being encouraged.

The above strategies and developments will clearly go some way to improving some of the practice concerns highlighted by these statistics. They are, however, not sufficient. Concern must exist that commitment to family support is not universal, and this can be highlighted by, for example, the large number of unplanned admissions and poor levels of parental access. The Regional Council clearly needs to re-affirm its commitment to family support and to ensure that this is clearly made known to *all* staff, who must then be held accountable for its implementation. The only way to move forward on these practice issues is to continue to emphasise prevention of family breakdown and ensure that only those children who need to be received into care actually come into care.

References

1. Strathclyde Regional Council. *Who Are They?* Social Work Department, 1981.

2. Demographic information extracted from Strathclyde Regional Council, Chief Executive's Department's mid-year estimates of population.

3. Social Work Services Group. *Children in Care and Under Supervision*. Annual bulletins.

4. Wedge, P. and Prosser, H. *Born to Fail?* Arrow Books, London, 1973.

5. Wedge, P. & Essen, J. *Children in Adversity*. Pan, London, 1982.

6. Roberts, G., Reinach, E. & Lovelock, R. *Children on the Rates*. Social Services Research and Intelligence Unit, Portsmouth, 1976.

7. Morgan-Klein, B. *Where am I Going to Stay?* Scottish Council for Single Homeless, Edinburgh, 1985.

8. Martin, F.M. & Murray, K. 'Achievements, Issues and Prospects'. In Martin, F.M. & Murray, K. *Children's Hearings*. Scottish Academic Press, Edinburgh, 1976.

9. Going for proof involves legally establishing the grounds for placing the child in care.

10. Packman, J. with Randall, J. & Jacques, N. *Who Needs Care? Social Work Decisions about Children*. Blackwell, Oxford, 1986.

11. Strathclyde Regional Council. 'Proposals for a Youth Strategy'. 1985.

12. *Social Work Decisions in Child Care: Recent Research Findings and Their Implications*. DHSS, HMSO, 1985.

13. Millham, S., Bullock, R., Hosie, H. & Haak, M. *Lost in Care*. Gower, Aldershot, 1986.

14. Strathclyde Regional Council. *Home or Away*. 1985.

15. Reinach, E. 'Decision making in Child Care'. In Reinach, E. (Ed.) *Decision Making in Child Care. Research Highlights*, No.1, Scottish Academic Press, Edinburgh, 1981.

16. Townsend, P. *Poverty in the United Kingdom*. Penguin, London, 1979.

17. Townsend, P. & Davidson, N. *Inequalities in Health* (the Black Report). Penguin, London, 1982.

18. Strathclyde Regional Council. Numerous internal papers providing referral analysis feedback to area teams 1981-87. See also Becker, S. and McPherson, S. 'Poor Clients'. University of Nottingham, 1986.

19. Fife Regional Council. *Unemployment and Referrals to the Regional Reporter*. 1986.

20. O'Toole, K. 'Theories,Professional Knowledge and Diagnosis of Child Abuse'. In Finkelhor, D., Gelles, R.J., Hotaling, G.T. & Straus, M.A. (Eds.) *The Darker Side of Families*. Sage, Beverley Hills, 1983.

Preventing Reception into Care: Monitoring a Short-Stay Refuge for Older Children

Moira Swanson

INTRODUCTION

Following McCluskey and Fegan's discussion of reception into care, this chapter looks briefly at some of the issues surrounding the reception into care of older children and at the development of one innovative resource designed to prevent family breakdown.

In Strathclyde Region attention was first focussed on the increasing proportion of older children being received into care when the preliminary findings of the Child Care Information System allowed comparison with figures contained in an earlier report issued in 1979 [1]. This showed that the percentage of children entering care aged 12-16 had risen from 30 per cent to almost 50 per cent. In order that appropriate preventive and diversionary schemes could be developed, the Department used the data collected through the information system to look at the family circumstances of older children coming into care and the reasons why admission was felt to be necessary.

Background Statistics

Analysis showed that fewer of the older children coming into care came from single parent families: across all age groups 26 per cent of children coming into care were living with both natural parents, 13 per cent being with a natural parent and a partner and 47 per cent with one natural parent. In the case of the older children the family composition was: with both parents, 49 per cent; with natural parent and partner, 19 per cent; with one natural parent, 32 per cent.

The main reasons for admission of older children in both 1984 and 1985 were found to be: being outwith parental control (28 per cent), truancy (20 per cent), offending (16 per cent) and a deteriorating relationship between child and carers (12 per cent).

Section 15 (voluntary care) was the most frequently used legislation (35 per cent), followed by Section 43 (4) (assessment) (22 per cent), Section 44(1)(b) (residential supervision) (19 per cent), and Section 37 (place of safety order) (10 per cent). On admission, 39 per cent went into children's homes, 43 per cent to Assessment Centres and 9 per cent to List D schools.

In *Lost in Care*, researchers from the Dartington Social Research Unit [2] describe a similar situation. With younger children the danger of neglect or the inability of the family to provide enduring and consistent care are the usual causes of long-term local authority care. With older children, by contrast, behaviour problems and unsatisfactory family relationships tend more often to be the important factors. Yet despite such problems the parents of older children are not disinterested in their care, as is shown in both the Dartington report and the study carried out in Sheffield by Fisher and his colleagues [3]. The fact that the parents had provided most or all of the care for the first ten years of their children's lives itself shows some degree of commitment.

The parents of the older children coming into care in Strathclyde were not generally unconcerned with the care of their children. In only 11 per cent of admissions did the parents wish no contact. Social workers were in fact more guilty of failing to acknowledge the importance of contact, despite the considerable attention paid to this topic over recent years [4,5], and recorded no details of access arrangements on 17 per cent of admission forms. Contact with other family members is also important if at least some degree of 'belonging' is to be maintained, yet in 66 per cent of cases no contact was arranged with relatives or no information on such contact was recorded.

The emerging picture suggested there was a significant number of young people coming into care for reasons apparently associated with their behaviour, from two-parent families, primarily on a voluntary basis, and with the parents wishing contact while their child was in care. In many cases they were being received into care for the first time despite long-term social work involvement. These findings led to a questioning of whether removal from the family home was an appropriate way to deal with such cases.

This question was felt to be especially important since several research projects have shown that the older the child, the more likely he or she will stay in care for a long period [2,6]. Our own figures bear this out. The following table compares the ages of the children received into care during the 12 months to March 1986 with the ages of those actually in care on the 31st March 1986. It can be seen that whereas only 51 per cent of admissions involved children aged 12 or over, fully 67 per cent of all those in care were in that category, suggesting a much higher 'turnover' of younger children.

TABLE 1

	Admissions during 12 months to 31st March 1986	In care at 31st March 1986
	%	%
0–4 years	28	10
5–8 years	11	10
8–11 years	10	13
12–15 years	49	48
16–17 years	2	19

Exploration of Issues

Through discussion and more detailed examination of individual cases, two problems were identified as being common. First, there is the trauma of adolescence itself, when young people criticise and test out themselves, their parents and their society. Secondly, there was often found to be a series of crises which had been building up over a period of time and had been brought to a head either by a legal infringement, or by the parent(s), or indeed the young person, reaching breaking point. Furthermore, difficulties in family relationships were often aggravated by the unemployment either of the parents or the young people. The Department was keen to develop resources which would enable such problems to be dealt with in ways which did not involve further deterioration in the relationship between the child and his or her family.

Family Rights

Views on how society should maintain a balance between the rights of parents and the welfare of children have been subject to changes in fashion over the years, influenced by the political climate, research [7,8] and individual events such as the death of children in care [9]. According to Adcock et al.

'… the pendulum has swung backwards and forwards between concern to protect and separate deprived children from their parents and concern to help and improve the circumstances of deprived parents so that they can care for their children' [10].

The debate continues, still affected by the political climate, especially the present emphasis on the family, research [11] and individual events such as again the death of a child in care [12] and more recently controversy over the identification of child abuse and the response to such identification [13].

Although the debate about parents' rights still appears to be of public interest, Fisher et al. [3] suggest that in reality parents themselves are less concerned about their rights and more concerned about fulfilling their moral responsibility towards their children. Reception into care, this study found, was viewed in terms of whether it made sense in terms of their moral responsibility rather than whether it affected their rights.

It was suggested that there was a frequent mismatch between parents' and social workers' perceptions of care. Parents were shown to regard their request for reception into care as a request for assistance with their child, not a denial of their responsibilities as parents. They often saw social workers' reluctance to admit as a belittlement of their problems, and as an implicit statement that in asking for help they were inadequate parents. The differences in perception often obstructed any preventive social work, as each participant was starting with a different view of what the problem was, what stage the crisis was at and what solution was required. What was perceived as a minor crisis by the social worker was often seen by the parents as the final straw of a string of crises. This was further complicated because when their child was admitted into care the parents experienced a sense of guilt, albeit tempered by relief that the problem was temporarily relieved.

Once their child was in care parents found difficulties in continuing their parenting roles and experienced a sense of disillusionment at what was happening to their child. They may have asked for help because of what they saw as unacceptable behaviour, for example, staying out late, smoking, bad language and associating with 'bad company', only to find this very behaviour when they visited the residential home. Also relevant and graphically described by the Dartington Social Research Unit [2] as well as by Fisher et al. [3], was the gradual loosening of parental ties which resulted from the inaccessability of the placement, lack of privacy during visits, lack of one steady figure with whom to discuss their child's progress, and an increasing feeling of powerlessness to affect what was actually happening.

Removing the child from home not only often makes the family's relationship problems worse, but also does little for the child. Children frequently have negative feelings about care [3,14,15,16,17]. The powerlessness felt by parents of children in care is also felt by the young people themselves [16]. For many there is a lack of preparation and explanation about going into care. Some are not consulted and only told they are going into care on the day it actually happens with no prior visit to the placement. Once in the home there is a lack of privacy and of the chance to be alone. There is little opportunity to talk to the staff on a one-to-one basis. Rules and regulations are not applied by all members of staff and the high turnover of staff makes it difficult to form relationships with them. The movement of children from home to home also prevents the forming of stable relationships. There is a high turnover of field social workers which also affects the continuity of care received by the child. Finally there are the educational problems experienced by many of the children which are aggravated by their being in care and their frequent change of school.

Prevention

Recognising the kinds of problems just outlined, many departments have been working towards a policy of 'non-residential care', and the closure of most children's homes. Warwickshire Social Services Department, for example, aims to close *all* children's homes [18]. This has demanded a radically different view of care. It has been impressed on all social work staff that substitute family care is the preferred option but that if at all possible children should be kept out of care. Few authorities would disagree with the stress on prevention, though many feel some form of residential care still to be appropriate.

Strathclyde's overall strategy of prevention referred to in the introduction involves a network of facilities. In the case of older children resources range from intermediate treatment and group work, which often have an explicit aim to reduce the number of children in danger of being received into care under compulsory measures, and Child and Family centres which work with a wider range of ages and problems. For some children, however, these services are not enough to alleviate the situation.

Older children usually have close ties with their families, however problematic, and many teenagers coming into care simply do not want surrogate families, particularly as foster placements are often outwith the young person's community. Finally, maintaining access can be just as difficult, or even more difficult, in fostering situations as in residential establishments as the Dartington study of access [3] and the chapter in this volume on temporary foster care show.

Recognising this, Strathclyde Regional Council initiated a new type of resource which, it was hoped, would not only prevent the breakdown of families and reception into care of older children, but would extend and develop appropriate supports for all young people with social problems. This resource would, it was hoped, provide support to children and families with relationship problems and not belittle these problems, but on the other hand would not encourage a relinquishing of parental responsibility and family breakdown. As this resource – a short-stay refuge – was the first of its kind, it was decided that it should be the subject of on-going monitoring and evaluation.

THE REFUGE

The refuge, made up of two maisonette flats converted into one house with a six-bedded facility, is within a complex comprising the area social work team, family centre and youth enquiry service, but services a wider area, and is staffed by two qualified social workers, six care staff and the project leader. It is operational on a 24 hour basis, seven days a week. It is essentially an out-of-hours service with regard to referrals, but for acute crisis situations is available at any time. It can provide either residential or non-residential respite care and intervention.

The work is based on a contract system between equal partners. This is an important element as it lays the responsibility for dealing with the problem on the young people and their families, with the refuge playing an advisory, supportive role. The contract may either be formally written or an informal agreement. No legislation is involved as it is felt that this would undermine the objective of preventing family breakdown and reception into care, and also that the frequently used Section 15 (Voluntary Care) is not appropriate legislation for 'children' who are essentially young adults.

Referrals can be made by Social Work, or any other agency, or directly by the young person or family members. All new referrals are dealt with by the qualified member of staff on duty, but wherever possible the care staff are also involved from the outset. The case is subsequently allocated at a management meeting, where issues such as personality, specific skills and current workload are considered. This consideration applies as much to the member of the care staff allocated to the case as to the qualified staff.

Those referred have often been low achievers at school and subject to negative influences both from within their own home and through the deprivation of their neighbourhood. In some cases they have suffered physical abuse or emotional neglect. Many of their families have experienced problems such as ill health, unemployment, poor housing conditions and marital breakdown, all of which have left a sense of failure and inadequacy which is often passed on to their children.

The method of working involves the staff visiting the home to discuss the family's difficulties. Siblings and other family members may join in the discussion with the young person and their parents, and this helps to let the family see itself as the means of its own solution. The role of the worker at this point is to encourage all family members to voice their perception of the problem. Once all concerned have had their say, each person is asked how they think the problem would best be resolved.

If a parent asks for the young person to be removed from home, the refuge worker will reply that this is not their role and that it would be for the parent to refer the child to the Reporter to the Children's Hearing, as being outwith parental control. The worker aims to establish a framework for conciliation, which might require residential or non-residential respite, or both. It is made clear that whatever is decided, involvement remains voluntary, and, in the case of residential respite, contracts are always signed by all concerned. Residential contracts emphasise the limited time-scale involved (48 hours) and the fact that it is not an in-care situation.

When summarising discussions, staff emphasise areas where agreement has been reached, even if this is as little as agreeing that a problem does exist and trying to find a means of resolving it. This at least is a basis to build on. This method allows both sides to be made aware of how the other feels. Young people often just say, 'I don't want to talk about it', or 'nobody ever listens', and parents that 'it's not worth talking to them – they think they know it all'. By encouraging discussion, feelings are brought out into the open, and hurts which have gone unnoticed are made apparent. By treating the opinions of the young person and family with respect, by emphasising any area of agreement, and by presenting the refuge as a mediator rather than 'a solver of problems' or an agent of control, staff try to give those involved a feeling of their ability to cope rather than reinforcing a sense of inadequacy, and they try to emphasise the reciprocity of the relationship between young person and parents.

This is not to say that problems have not been encountered by using this approach. Bringing anger out into the open and allowing both sides equal status can cause resentment; for example, if parents do not concede that their child has rights, opinions, beliefs, they may see the refuge as taking sides with the young person and even encouraging the rebellion. Such a family may expect the refuge to back them up, to discipline their 'unruly child', and when this is not done it may seem like letting the young person off. Conversely, the young person may see the refuge as taking the family's side, or at the other extreme they may try to use the refuge as a weapon with which to get at the family. Clearly, a high level of sensitivity and tact has to be employed by the staff.

MONITORING OF THE REFUGE

Much attention has been paid in recent years to questions of the role of evaluative research within social services [19,20], the manner in which it should be carried out, and the validity of its findings. Many research projects have been criticised for lacking clear objectives and for producing more questions than answers. But while to a point these criticisms have been justified, they often stem from an overly idealised view of the nature of scientific research – a view which is increasingly questioned by researchers.

Smith and Cantley [21], for example, argue that such an 'ideal' view rests upon naive assumptions about the nature of social services organisations, in particular that they have explicitly formulated aims and objectives laid down by management and understood and shared by practitioners. They reject the underlying premise that organisations can be explained by 'functionalist' social theory (which presupposes a high degree of integration) and they wish, rather, to emphasise the plurality of interests and perspectives typically encountered.

The main task of the research undertaken on the refuge to date and described here, was to monitor the early stages of the project's development and describe how its original aims and objectives were clarified through experience. Given that this was the first resource of this type within the region, it was important to monitor its setting up and thus ensure that when similar resources were developed in other areas they could build on this experience. The monitoring therefore was concerned with looking at the development of the project as a whole. It did not attempt to identify the objectives of intervention nor to evaluate the outcome on an individual case basis. The first stage attempted to identify the perceptions of those involved of the aims and objectives attached to the refuge.

Perception of Objectives

It quickly became clear that different levels of staff held quite different views. For senior management the principal objective was to prevent family breakdown, thereby reducing the number of children being received into care and the number of young single homeless people presenting at the department. As the refuge offered respite care, it was expected that the bed spaces would be used as part of the crisis intervention process. It was also envisaged that outreach work would be undertaken, perhaps in conjunction with other street-based workers already in post. Finally, this group hoped that refuge workers would take a lead role in coordinating the efforts of other agencies (such as housing, education, Department of Health and Social Security (DHSS), and other social work sections) into a more coherent approach to young people's problems.

Preventing family breakdown and reception into care was the primary aim for middle management too, but with a greater emphasis on evaluation. For this group it was important to measure the effectiveness of the processes and practices employed, to compare the refuge's work with other types of intervention, and to study the responses of the consumers.

Project staff agreed on the primacy of preventing family breakdown and admission to care, but stressed that achieving this would depend on establishing integrated interagency responses. They recognised the need for reactive crisis-intervention work, while emphasising the desirability of a more pro-active approach.

Thus far, general views were compatible, albeit with differing emphases. However, divergent views were held by the final key group of protagonists – the three senior social workers in the local area team, together with the project leader of the Family Centre with whom they liaised closely. They saw the role of the refuge as preventing reception into care, not only in terms of a reactive, crisis-intervention role, but in a proactive approach involving participation in various strategies already operated by the teams, for example, community-based alternatives to List D schools. In terms of the work of the refuge staff, this would have meant providing a supervisory, day-care type of service, which they felt would be restrictive and would limit them to providing merely another 'gatekeeping' resource. There were also professional differences between the social work and refuge staff regarding the methodology employed by the refuge. Any attempt to monitor the refuge had to acknowledge these differing perspectives.

Further Monitoring

The second stage of the monitoring involved spending time examining case records so that a picture could be built up of the type and diversity of the problems experienced by those referred to the refuge. The results of this analysis are summarised below. During this stage a lot of time was spent observing, in what was initially a non-participatory manner. This was felt to be of prime importance as it allowed the researcher to become known and accepted by all involved. It also allowed the relationships between staff, parents and young people to be examined. The role of the researcher was explained fully to all participants.

The third stage involved identifying and interviewing key participants. Initially it was hoped that it would be possible to avoid sampling, and to interview all participants, but as the flow of referrals increased it was decided to formally interview an age-stratified sample of young people, and where relevant their parents and social workers, and to cover the rest of those involved by informal discussion. This stage had to be extended as the work of the refuge developed and expanded. It became necessary to include the views of representatives of other agencies, such as the District Council Housing Department, DHSS, Education and Police, as well as other participants in the project, such as residential staff and providers of supported lodging placements.

Some of the results of the second two stages of the research are described below.

The First Year's Referrals

During its first year the refuge had 134 referrals, including six alerts for missing persons, and 15 categorised as inappropriate. Forty-nine per cent of clients were aged under 16, while those aged 16 accounted for 31 per cent. Almost two-thirds of the total had experienced some kind of social work involvement prior to referral to the refuge. All the young people had relationship difficulties with their carers. These varied from fairly typical problems of adolescence to more deeply rooted relationship problems, often linked to marital breakdown, emotional instability of the carer, or alcohol abuse by the carer. Other presenting problems were; homelessness, beyond parental control, violence in the home, school related problem, alcohol usage, solvent abuse, offence related problems and problems related to residential care.

Excluding referrals there were 89 clients receiving a service from the refuge. 19 received only advice. Of the remaining 70, 15 entered into a non-residential contract and 26 a residential contract. The remaining 29 were offered support and counselling on a non-contractual basis.

What happened to the 70 young people who received more than advice after the period of intervention? At the time of survey, 54 were still at their parent's home, of whom three had first gone into supported lodgings or bed and breakfast accommodation and one had gone into care. Eight were in supported lodgings, five in bed and breakfast accommodation and one in the District Council Homeless Unit. A further five had their own tenancy, all having been helped towards this by the refuge. All those outwith the family home continue to receive support. Indeed there are plans to form a young tenants' association in order to support other young people moving into their own homes, both by giving advice regarding DHSS help, and by building up a pool of necessary decorating implements and DIY tools.

Seven of the young people dealt with by the refuge went into residential care. All had prior social work involvement, which in three instances could be said to have been long term. Indeed, one was in foster care at the time of referral.

Homelessness

A key development in the life of the refuge was its focus on the issue of homelessness. To date, the refuge has dealt with 26 homeless young people. Contrary to the belief of some housing and social work staff, the research found that young people did not leave home for little reason and without thought, but to escape violence or emotional conflict. The number who chose to remain outwith the family home after experiencing the trauma of homelessness indicated how strongly they must feel.

Initially, most referrals came from social work staff and involved young people under 16 years of age. The service requested tended to be counselling and support and when accommodation was offered, it was normally of a respite nature. However, as the refuge became widely known, there was an increase in self-referrals, which came more from young people over 16. In working with this group refuge workers rapidly became aware of the lack of long term accommodation for young people. The relationship beween the Housing Department and the Social Work Department at that time was generally poor, and disputes arose over the implementation of the Homeless Persons Act.

Only a few months after becoming operational, the refuge staff found themselves housing four teenagers with nowhere else to go. All had applied to the District Council Housing Department under the 1977 Homeless Persons Act, but their applications had been refused on the grounds that they were not vulnerable. Some sort of action was felt necessary as the refuge could not provide accommodation on a long term basis.

On the advice of Shelter, two of the teenagers sought legal advice. Following this, with great reluctance all four teenagers were given ten days notice to quit, after which one moved into the District Council Homeless Unit and three were found commercial bed and breakfast accommodation. The two girls went on to appear in court and a decision was given in their favour. This decision, which detailed the Housing Department's responsibilities towards homeless teenagers, to a great extent shaped the direction of the work of the refuge in the months to come. One of the boys eventually returned to his parents' home, the two girls were given their own homes, and the other boy was still, at the time of the survey, in supported lodgings awaiting housing. The following case study provides an example.

Gemma, aged 16

Gemma was referred to social work by her teacher after she had been put out of the family home. The Area Team passed the referral on to the refuge.

She stayed at the refuge on three occasions, when, despite attempts by staff, family problems reached crisis point once more. She was eventually evicted from her family home half an hour before her 16th birthday. She then stayed at the refuge and was one of the group, just described, who applied to the Housing Department for a house of her own, was refused and eventually took legal action against the District Council. She was given accommodation in the Homeless Unit while awaiting the court case, after which she was allocated a District Council flat.

I asked Gemma about what had happened over the last year:

Family:- 'I never want to see them again and I don't think I'll change my mind about this although I miss my wee brother.'

The Court Case:- 'I was frightened, it was a brass neck standing there, but I knew I had to do it if I wanted a house – everybody was dead nice though!'

Social Work:- 'It's if you get into trouble. I didn't – I've not got a social worker, my dad did!'

Refuge:- 'Great! There should be one everywhere for young folk in trouble. The staff are good – I mean they can get mad with you, but they're good and friendly and help you. They listen to you and don't shout.'

Own House:- 'I'm OK now I like it and I've got good neighbours, they help me – the staff from the refuge came in and I come here. Val helps to budget and things.'

Work:- 'I had a job in Fine Fare, but I hated the crowds and it was too busy. I'd like a job in a wee shop, not a big supermarket.'

The Past Year:- 'Sometimes it was hellish, but I think it's OK now. I know what it's like being on your own so I'm not so scared. I wasn't grown up then, but I am now.'

Would you do it again:- 'Yes I would, I'd have done it. But I don't know if I'd have managed without the refuge, I'd have had to sleep rough – I'd done that before and I wouldn't have known what to do with the Housing Department or the Social. Nobody should have to sleep rough or stay with folk. There should be a refuge and a homeless unit, but it has to be in a good bit – they always put us in bad areas.'

Not all the cases involving homelessness were as dramatic as the two involving court proceedings, but all involved vulnerable young people in need of help. A further example of work in this field is provided by the following case study.

Sandra – 17

Sandra was told about the refuge by a friend when she was trying to get into the Homeless Unit. She had kept house for her father since her mother died. She went into care for a spell and then went back to her father. It didn't work out and she felt forced to leave home. She still keeps in touch with her father, but doesn't want to live with him. The refuge provides advice and support and she just wants somewhere to come where there is no hassle. These are Sandra's comments:

Family:- 'It was OK till my mum died then it was hopeless. I went into a children's home. It was OK I suppose, but I didn't really like it. I got back home, but it just got worse. I couldn't stay with him.'

Homeless Unit:- 'It's OK, but it's dirty and there's always fights. A lot of folk hang about the place – like folk's husbands.'

Social Work:- 'The thing about social work is they've never got any time. They're always dead busy or else they don't come when they say they will, maybe they can't help it.'

Refuge:- 'It's a good idea. I wish I'd known about it before. I like coming here on a Thursday and I like the staff, they're dead helpful.

Work:- 'You can't get a job, it's hopeless. I'm trying to go into nursing, that's what I really want.'

Future:- I think I'll be OK. I'm good with money and I know how to look after a house. I don't think I'll be lonely, I've got some friends. I'm looking forward to getting my house, but the Housing are dead slow.'

What is there for teenagers who need help and advice:- 'Not much – and you don't know who to ask. My Social Worker is nice but she's too busy. You need a place like the refuge to help you with things like housing and the Social.' Work ongoing with the Housing Department should ensure that in the future there will be adequate provision for young homeless but they will still need support. It is hoped that the housing provision made will take the form of more supported accommodation and shared tenancies as well as mainstream housing for those young people who are assessed as being mature enough to cope with living alone. The assessment and supervisory aspect would be shared jointly by Refuge and Housing staff.

CONCLUSION

Almost all the individuals and agencies who were interviewed were positive about the refuge and saw the value of this type of resource. A full report on the work of the refuge which, it is hoped, will be of use to managers and practitioners setting up similar resources, is available from the department [22]. The project leader also discusses the work of the project in a number of published sources [23]. Below is a very brief summary of the project's strengths and weaknesses. Further research looking at outcomes on an individual case basis is planned.

The refuge successfully provided a service which catered for the needs of both under and over 16 year olds coming with a variety of problems which were in the main related to the normal problems of adolescence although often exacerbated by additional family relationship problems. Situations where the refuge was unable to prevent family breakdown were generally where the person was under 16, had a longstanding relationship problem with their carers and school-related problems. In many of these cases there had been long-term social work involvement and a variety of strategies had been tried. The refuge was unable to provide the day care support with educational input needed by these young people and without this the danger of their ending up in List D or List G provision was great.

The refuge became caught up in the issue of homelessness primarily because it became involved with some young people with longstanding relationship problems but also simply because the problem was there. It dealt with homelessness in an innovative way which has had implications not only for its own district but for other local authority housing departments. All of the young people referred due to homelessness have been reconciled with their families although they may not be sharing a house with them. Where reconciliation has been achieved the work of the refuge can be described as successful. The work of the refuge is clearly in line with the views emerging from recent research in England and Wales [11] and with current discussion of child care law emphasising prevention in the broader sense of preventing family breakdown rather than the narrow sense of preventing reception into care.

The refuge was given freedom to respond to the needs of the area and this flexibility contributed to its success. A similar resource set up in another area may require to respond to different issues and thus develop in a different way. Although it does appear that flexibility is an advantage it can result in problems if those involved in the project are not clear about its aims and objectives. Lack of clarity leads to inappropriate referrals and disappointment in the service given. More discussion between those directly and indirectly involved in the project has helped. Future projects, it is hoped, would promote such discussion at an early stage.

References

1. *Who Are They?* Strathclyde Regional Council, Social Work Department, 1981.

2. Millham, S., Bullock, R., Hosie, H. and Haak, M. *Lost in Care*. Gower, Aldershot, 1986.

3. Fisher, M., Marsh, P., Phillip, D. with Sainsbury, E. *In and Out of Care*. Batsford, London, 1986.

4. Johnson, D. 'Access: the Natural Parents' Dilemma' *Adoption and Fostering*. 10, 3, 1986.

5. Gibson, P. and Parsloe, P. 'What Stops Parental Access' *Adoption and Fostering*. 8, 1, 1984.

6. Vernon, J. & Fruin, D. *In Care*. National Children's Bureau, London, 1986.

7. Rowe, J. & Lambert, L. *Children Who Wait*. Association of British Adoption Agencies, London, 1973.

8. Goldstein, J., Freud, A. & Solnit, J. *Beyond the Best Interests of the Child*. Collier MacMillan, London, 1973.

9. *Report to the Committee of Inquiry into the Care and Supervision Provided in Relation to Maria Colwell*. HMSO, London, 1974.

10. Adcock, M., White, R. & Rowlands, O. *The Administrative Parent*. British Agencies for Adoption and Fostering, London, 1983.

11. *Social Work Decisions in Child Care: Recent Research Findings and their Implications*. DHSS, HMSO, London, 1985.

12. *A Child in Trust* (Inquiry into Beckford Case). London Borough of Brent, 1986.

13. For example, the inquiry into responses to child abuse in Cleveland, due to report in 1988.

14. *Children in Homes*. Child Care Study Paper No.3, Church of England Children's Society, 1979.

15. Stein, M. and Carey, K. *Leaving Care*. Basil Blackwell, London, 1986.

16. Morgan-Klein, B. *Where am I Going to Stay?* Scottish Council for Single Homeless, Edinburgh, 1985.

17. Berridge, D. *Children's Homes*. Blackwell, London, 1985.

18. Harbridge, E. 'The Last of the Residential Homes' *Community Care*. 18, September, 1986.

19. Lishman, J. (Ed.) *Evaluation, 2nd edition. Research Highlights* No.8, Jessica Kingsley, London, 1988.

20. Sheldon, B. 'Social Work Effectiveness Experiments: Review and Implications' *British Journal of Social Work*. April, 1986.

21. Smith, G. & Cantley, C. 'Pluralistic Evaluation'. In Lishman, J. (Ed.) *Evaluation, 2nd edition. Research Highlights* No.8, Jessica Kingsley, London, 1988.

22. *Short Stay Refuge*. Strathclyde Regional Council, 1987.

23. Cran, J. 'A Refuge for Young People' *The Scottish Child*. Issue No.12, Summer, 1986.

Preventing Reception into Care: Monitoring an Initiative Using Section 12 Funds

Richard Fowles

INTRODUCTION

This chapter describes a project set up in Strathclyde to try to prevent family breakdown through the provision of financial assistance. Like the chapter on the short-stay refuge it provides an example of the in-house monitoring exercises which require to be set up when new initiatives are developed.

In 1984 Strathclyde Regional Council introduced a preventive initiative using assistance under Section 12 in order to help keep together families where a high risk of children coming into care had been identified. Section 12 of the Social Work (Scotland) Act, 1968, sets out in law the responsibility of local authority social work departments 'to promote social welfare by making available advice, guidance and assistance on such a scale as may be appropriate for their area' [1]. It also specifies to whom such assistance can be provided and in particular refers to 'a person, being a child under the age of eighteen, requiring assistance in kind, or in exceptional circumstances cash, where such assistance appears to the local authority to diminish the need to receive him into, or keep him in care.'

Differing views on the role of financial aid in social work have always existed. Jackson and Valencia [2], reviewing the situation in 1979, saw the use at that time as largely being crisis intervention, and they suggested that the preventive and promotional use of financial aid should be developed.

> 'Preventive work means that social workers would give aid not to meet an immediate crisis but to forestall development of such a situation in the future (in the past it has been expressed as taking action which would avoid greater expense to the local authority in the future); promotional work would allow social workers to take action which would lift clients and groups above contemporary minimum standards (such as the provision of

holidays, payment of fees for pre-school play groups or music lessons) and to assist in community development.'

They feared, however, that there would be little development in the positive use of Section 12. For many years social work departments have been able to provide material and financial assistance in order to prevent the reception of children into care and promote social welfare. Although the extent to which Section 12 has been used as a means of social work intervention has varied, even between neighbouring social work area teams [2,3,4], the fact remains that it has been used on countless occasions over the years. Why, then, did Strathclyde Regional Council decide to introduce a special initiative in 1984?

BACKGROUND TO THE SCHEME

Two principal factors underpinned the thinking of the initiative. First was the Council's strongly held belief that the most appropriate environment in which children should grow up is that of their natural family. Social work intervention should be aimed at supporting children and their parents so that they can remain together. Children should only be received into public care when for them to remain with their parents would demonstrably be inconsistent with their welfare [5]. Second was an awareness that poverty and material deprivation all too often play a part in the crises, the breakdown of relationships, and the stresses which lead to children being received into care. Similarly, it was not uncommon for a family's attention to be so concentrated on financial and material pressures that both they and their social worker were unable to focus on relationship difficulties and inappropriate family functioning. Although advice on debt management, and liaison with other statutory bodies usually managed to prevent a threatened eviction or disconnection of fuel supply, in many cases this was little more than short term respite which provided a little breathing space before the next crisis arrived.

Council members and officials were aware of and had access to numerous research reports showing how, on many indicators, such as health, physical development, housing and school performance, children from a background of poverty and disadvantage differed from the general child population [6]. With regard to children in poverty, three main categories of family can be easily identified: the unemployed, the low paid and the single parent family. The numbers of children in these groups, nationally and within Strathclyde, have been increasing over the past ten years [7,8,9,10].

The incidence of poverty is not evenly spread. Indicators of deprivation (e.g. unemployment, single parent families, housing lacking basic amenities) from the

1981 Census showed clearly that poverty and deprivation are concentrated in particular urban areas. In April 1984 the picture in Strathclyde [11] showed 17.5 per cent of the 'working' population was unemployed, compared with 15.1 per cent in Scotland as a whole, and 12.8 per cent in Great Britain. Concentrations of male unemployment of 50 per cent were noted in parts of the East End of Glasgow and in designated 'areas for priority treatment' (APTs), such as Ferguslie Park in Paisley. A similar pattern of concentration occurs with single parents [7]. Whereas nationally, some 12 per cent of children live in single parent families, the figure for Strathclyde is 15.5 per cent. For Glasgow it is 21.3 per cent, and it is higher still for some of the Region's APTs, with Ferguslie Park, for instance, at 28.4 per cent.

Within the context of the general studies of the effect of poverty on children, research was also taking place both within and outwith Strathclyde which confirmed that those living in families experiencing poverty and deprivation were more likely to be received into care than other children. It was the recognition of these findings which was most relevant in providing the impetus and rationale for the Section 12 initiative.

Wedge and Essen [6] had shown that, by the age of 16, 16 per cent of disadvantaged children had experience of being in care, compared to two per cent of other 16-year-olds. And of course, local statistics have been available for some time which point to an association between admission to care and several poverty indicators, such as dependence upon state benefit and membership of large families or single parent families [12].

Although not all poverty is found within socially deprived areas, there are strong indications that a disproportionate number of children received into care come from geographic areas of social deprivation. Children in Strathclyde's APTs are four times more likely to be taken into care than children from areas of the Region with fewer social problems. This finding is supported by other research. A study in Portsmouth [13] found that over two-thirds of the children received into care were drawn from just five of the city's 16 wards. These five tended to be those with the highest proportion of unskilled manual workers, lone parents, and inadequate housing.

From these circumstances of deprivation, problems, often of a very practical nature, can arise which in turn may lead to family breakdown and the removal of children from their families. Inadequate housing in areas where turnover of families is rapid means that there are few family and community supports available. Low income, a significant strain in itself, leads to debt, lack of necessary resources, and of opportunity for relaxation, stimulation or learning. Lack of respite, for parents and children, where the finance and the opportunity are not available, leads to friction and strain on family relationships. All these problems combine to cause stress on families who lack the resources to cope, and the risk of family breakdown and of the children being received into care is substantially increased.

The Council's commitments to preventing reception into care and to rehabilitation have already been outlined in chapter two. Given the evidence just reviewed, those commitments were clearly consistent with the broader 'social strategy' within which Council policies aimed at discrimination in favour of areas of disadvantage in order to ameliorate socially depriving conditions. The theme of preventive work in situations of deprivation was therefore emphasised in the social work department's contribution to the review of the wider deprivation stategy. This included a commitment to reduce the rates of poverty-related admissions. One course of action proposed as a means of achieving this was by extending the Section 12 budget, and the Section 12 preventive initiative was born from this proposal.

As said at the beginning of this chapter, the Social Work (Scotland) Act, 1968, refers particularly to the provision of assistance in kind or cash to prevent children being received into care. However, although Section 12 assistance had been used over the years in this manner, payments had been comparatively small and though they had dealt with the immediate crisis, they had done little or nothing to tackle the wider, general problems of poverty and deprivation faced by families.

The purpose of the preventive initiative was to allow Section 12 to be used in a more coordinated and imaginative manner. Families would be identified where there was considered to be a high risk of the children being received into care and where material deprivation and financial problems were seen as being an integral part of that risk. Section 12 finances could be used in greater amounts than had been the normal practice in the past, to support and enhance the casework input to the families, as a means of keeping the families intact. The initiative would also be applied in cases where children currently in care would be more likely to be rehabilitated to their families as a result of financial support being made available. Jackson and Valencia [2], discussing the development of the use of financial aid in England and in Scotland, suggest that it was the Ingleby Committee [14] which acted as a catalyst. The Strathclyde initiative, although involving large sums, was clearly in line with the Ingleby Committee's acceptance of the social work organisations' view that

'... for the effective prevention of suffering of children through neglect in their own homes a skilled intensive case-work service was required (provided either directly by local authorities or through a voluntary agency) and that local authorities should have power to give material assistance where necessary.'

It moves away from the use of financial aid in a reactive manner [4].

It was also considered that the initiative might demonstrate that prevention of admission to care was not only the most desirable goal in terms of childcare practice, but also the most cost-effective form of intervention. The report of the Parliamentary Select Committee on Social Services entitled, 'Children in Care' [15] itself stated that 'such small specific grants are hardly luxuries in the context of costs of the child care system.' The cost of having a child in care is normally estimated at around £3,000 per year, and it should be noted that in Strathclyde at the present time the portion of the Section 12 budget devoted to the prevention of reception into care is some one per cent of the budget for children in care.

THE PILOT PROJECT

In early 1984 a pilot project was initiated involving seventeen families nominated by Area Offices from existing caseloads. These families met the two criteria for inclusion into the scheme, first, there should either be children in care at present, who could be rehabilitated to their family, or a high risk that children presently with their families, might need to be received into care; and secondly, there should be a substantial element of poverty contributing to the childcare problem.

The amount of money set aside for each case was based on an initial estimate by the Area Office concerned of the likely amount needed to meet their objectives with the respective families. Sums ranging from £750 to £5,000 were allocated to each family, although the most actually spent was £2,500.

The pilot project was closely monitored and in November 1984 an interim report was considered by the Social Work (Development) Sub-Committee. This report indicated that the project had been a success; in none of the cases had there been a deterioration in the family's circumstances, despite, in some instances, horrifying developments such as the death of a single parent, leaving a teenage son, with a lengthy history of List D School attendance, in the care of an older sister. Out of the 17 families, who were all selected because of the high risk of breakdown and separation, there was only one instance of reception into care. This was a result of a Children's Hearing decision, against the social worker's recommendation and related to offences committed prior to the start of the initiative.

One of the families included in the pilot project was a young married couple with five children under eight years of age. All five were on the 'At Risk' register and had been received into care briefly in September 1983 following a child abuse investigation. Over the years, there had been repeated instances of concern at the low standards of child care. Material conditions within the home were very poor. The father had been unemployed for several years and the children's development was slow because of a lack of stimulation. Both parents often felt depressed, and family morale had been at a consistently low ebb with frequent financial crises. The family was isolated in the area where they lived, and had been ostracised by their neighbours. It was the view of the Area Office workers that the family was at considerable risk of breakdown and the children in danger of being received into care.

The objectives of the preventive initiative were to promote a housing transfer, improve material conditions in the home and provide greater facilities for play and stimulation for the children. By the time of the interim report in November 1984, the housing authority had agreed to a transfer, and the family had moved to a semi-detached house in an area specifically chosen because of the support facilities available locally, such as a community worker, well known to the family, and a Child and Family Centre. Finance to the total of £1,586 was spent on household equipment, clothing and playthings, to supplement those items provided by the DHSS. Further expenditure was planned to provide an inexpensive holiday, which would be the family's first ever, and to install a shower, both for reasons of economy, and to assist in getting the children prepared for school in the mornings.

This, along with other examples, led the interim report to conclude that:

> 'Obviously, with family problems as deep rooted and intractable as these, quick and simplistic conclusions would be inappropriate. However, in terms of the impetus given to good social work practice, as well as in terms of the intended result – keeping children out of care – the initial conclusions are encouraging.'

The report was approved and the decision taken to extend the Initiative across Strathclyde.

THE MAIN INITIATIVE

Since it was proposed that Section 12 would be used 'in greater amounts than has been normal practice in the past', the initiative itself was potentially something of a political hot potato from the start. It was easy to see how the initiative might be portrayed by those not in agreement with or sympathetic towards its underlying philosophy. The obvious charge would be that the department was lavishing large sums of ratepayers' money on bad, unreliable and inadequate parents, some of whom had already had their children taken from them and received into care. Why should these parents be rewarded for their failure by having their houses redecorated and being paid to go on holiday?

Given that many of the families had already been in receipt of a social work service for a number of years, apparently to little or no positive effect, it might also be argued that the decision to spend public funds on them was based more on desperation than sound judgement. Would this money not be better spent on services and resources for those generally perceived as being 'deserving', for instance, the mentally or physically handicapped? How would other clients of the Social Work Department perceive the initiative? Would they not start to demand similar financial assistance for themselves and their families?

From the start there was considerable anxiety that the initiative would attract adverse comment and publicity in the media. Concern over how the initiative would be seen if it had not been subject to scrutiny by elected members resulted in its being taken to the social work committee in February 1984. Senior management staff were instructed to carry out an immediate review of all the cases on the pilot project to confirm that the families met the criteria and to ensure the standard of practice was of a high order. The social work committee itself also laid down certain conditions to be applied in all the cases. These conditions formed the basis of operational procedures applied from then onwards.

Although procedures exist to cover many areas of social work practice, and all recognise the need for accountability and supervision, the detailed nature of the Section 12 Preventive Initiative Procedures and the extent of the supervisory role given to senior management reflects the department's awareness to the sensitivity of the initiative itself. While the close control of operation and administration was partly designed to ensure a high standard of practice, it was also aimed at preventing any laxity which would provide examples of what might be perceived as extravagance by those unsympathetic to the initiative.

The practice instruction note given to staff emphasised the legal authority for the use of Section 12 finance and that the usual principles governing the use of Section 12 should also apply to the initiative. For instance Section 12 should not be used as a form of additional income maintenance, nor should it supplant the responsibilities of the DHSS or any other statutory agency. The client should participate fully in the decision-making process and should not become over-dependent on financial aid. Section 12 payments should not be provided as a substitute for other necessary forms of social work involvement. When a family was put forward as being suitable for the initiative, the Divisional Director was responsible for ensuring that the criteria were satisfied.

During the actual period of financial input the District Manager was required to review the case on a monthly basis, the Area Officer to carry out a fortnightly review to monitor expenditure, and the Senior Social Worker was expected to supervise the case on a weekly basis. Section 12 money was not to be used on the purchase of 'luxury' items: these were not defined, but District Managers, in consultation with the Divisional Director if necessary, were given the responsibility to determine and prevent expenditure of this nature. Only in exceptional cases was Section 12 to be used to pay off arrears or debts. Normally advocacy was to be used to arrange more favourable payments. Cash was not normally to be given directly to the family unless in small amounts and unless specified in the original application.

Although the need for careful procedures of accountability and the highest standards of accompanying social work practice was generally accepted, there was a feeling in some Area Offices that the actual procedures laid down were somewhat excessive. (Interestingly, during the actual period of financial assistance the review procedure is more demanding than that laid down in the department's child abuse procedures, and entails more regular direct involvement on the part of senior management personnel). Indeed, there was some concern that the procedural demands would inhibit the type of family casework the initiative was designed to facilitate. Although difficult to substantiate, it is also possible that the awareness of these demands has acted as a disincentive for social workers when considering whether to nominate one of the families on their caseload.

MONITORING

From the start it was recognised that the initiative should be monitored, both as a matter of good practice, and as a means of gauging its effectiveness. Given its innovatory nature and concern about possible opposition, monitoring was also important. The differing views of social workers about the validity of using Section 12 as part of casework have been well documented [2,3,4]. If it could be demonstrated that the initiative was succeeding in its aims of preventing reception into care and helping ensure the rehabilitation of children already in care, any criticism could be answered.

However, there are considerable difficulties in evaluating a project of this sort [16]. There is no means of knowing for certain what would have happened to the families had the additional resources not been available. There could be no control group of comparative families not receiving social work assistance as this would run contrary to a professional and legal duty to assist all families who require support and advice.

Monitoring of the initiative has therefore taken a descriptive form. Information was obtained from interviews with the social workers and other staff involved. Starting with an initial profile of each family and its difficulties, with an assessment of future prospects and anticipated problems, the course of social work and financial input was charted. The effects of this were noted, and by relating outcome back to the initial assessment of the family and the future, some conclusions could be drawn as to what contribution the special initiative may have made. Inevitably this picture is a subjective one, based primarily on the perceptions of the fieldwork staff involved.

In 1985/86 17 families received assistance, involving a total of 47 children. Of the families, nine were single parents (two male, seven female) and eight were couples. None had an adult in employment.

In the case of two families it proved necessary for the children to be received into care. In each of these the number of children was two, and in both instances the separation is seen as long term. In percentage terms this means that, taking admission to care as a crude indicator of success or failure, the initiative was successful with 88 per cent of the families or 91 per cent of the children. This can be considered as a very satisfactory outcome, especially given that the families were, by definition, at high risk of breakdown. (This conclusion clearly hinges on the accuracy of social workers' initial assessments that the families were at risk).

Family size varied from one child to six children.

No. of children	No. of cases
1	2
2	8
3	3
4	2
6	2

The parental factors which were seen as creating vulnerability were identified for all the families (several of its factors were often present in each case).

Debt	5
Depression/Psychiatric Illness	7
Neglect of Children	7
Housing Problems	6
Alcohol Abuse	5
Lack of Stimulation for Children	5
Lack of Control of Children	5
Child Abuse	3
Mental Handicap	3
Marital Stress	2

The total funds allocated to these cases were £18,475 (grants) and £750 (loans) (an average of £409 per child). The total actually spent amounted to £17,008 (an average of £361.78 per child). Bearing in mind the annual cost of maintaining a child in care, the cost effectiveness is apparent, let alone the personal and social benefits to the families.

The type of expenditure fell under the following categories:

Debt (credit/catalogues	£2028)	
(rent arrears	£1234)	
(fuel	£ 810)	£ 4,072
Household furnishings and equipment		£10,007
Clothing		£ 1,005
Books, toys, educational costs		£ 625
Holidays, travel, outings		£ 1,248

Interviews were conducted with all the social workers involved with the families. The comments made by the social workers also provided a positive picture of the initiative's effectiveness and the progress made by the families as a result. Although, as said earlier, it is impossible to assess with complete certainty what would have happened to the families if they had not been included in the initiative, the fact that virtually all the social workers considered that there had been either some or substantial improvement in their individual family's circumstances makes it difficult to avoid an encouraging conclusion about the effectiveness of the scheme.

Even in one of the two cases where the children were received into care the social worker commented that the family's inclusion in the project was worthwhile. The parents were both described as being mildly mentally handicapped with the mother suffering from depression. Their lifestyle was chaotic, their parenting skills limited and the children were seen as being understimulated. In addition to ongoing work with the family, £1,500 was spent on household equipment. However, deterioration in the mother's mental condition resulted in the two young children being received into care for a three month period and a further admission two months later following abuse of one of the children. Despite this the social worker considered that:

> 'The financial input was a positive resource which had to be used in an attempt to avoid reception into care. It enabled a relatively nomadic family to maintain a home and allowed considerable social work support to be given to the family ... we have the unusual situation of a family having come to terms with their difficulties and agreeing that now there is no other course but adoption.'

There were only two cases where the aim was to restore the children to their parents' care. In both cases this objective was achieved. In the first case this involved two children who had been in care for five years. The parents had been homeless and their lack of control of the children was seen as a principal cause of the reception into care. £1,308 was spent, £360 on rent arrears to facilitate the allocation of a new house and £948 on furnishings. The two teenage children were discharged from care and a year later the family situation was described as stable. The second case involved a male single parent with three children. There was concern about the father's use of alcohol and his ability to cope with the children. In fact because of this the daughter was living with relatives. The boys were exhibiting severe attendance and behaviour difficulties at school. The financial input was spent on furnishing and decorating materials, clothing and a family holiday. The father's self-esteem and confidence increased significantly, the daughter returned home and relationships within the family strengthened.

Many of the social workers referred to the way that the use of Section 12 finance on this scale had significantly alleviated parental stress and anxiety. This in turn usually resulted in the parents taking a more active and more appropriate involvement with their children and in a more stable home environment in general. This can be seen in the case of a female single parent with three children under five who, when nominated for the initiative, was seen as being tired, depressed and isolated. There was concern at the lack of stimulation provided to the children and their slow development. In total £970 was spent on household equipment, toys, clothing and debt. As a result the mother was seen as becoming brighter and more self-assured. She became less isolated through involvement in community groups, the level of care offered to the children improved and their own development became more appropriate for their ages. The social worker concluded, 'The possibility of these children being removed into care now appears remote.'

Several workers also commented that the use of Section 12 funding allowed them to start to make progress on a casework basis, where formerly this had been virtually impossible as the family's attention had been focussed on financial crisis:

> 'The money that has been spent on the family has done much to boost their morale and thereby has made the professional Social Work intervention more effective.'

> 'The Section 12 Initiative provided the worker with a timely boost and allowed for a new range of treatment options by providing for the first time the tools to deal with the long recognised social and economic problem.'

Given that all the families were perceived as being at a high risk of breakdown it is not surprising that spectacular progress was not achieved in every case. Although diminished, relationship difficulties often remained and concern about the possibility of reception into care was not completely removed. When commenting on the situation of a female single parent with two sons of primary school age, the social worker, while acknowledging some improvement, also stated that

> 'none of this was achieved smoothly as the mother's emotional and personal difficulties detract from her ability to cooperate fully.'

The fact that in virtually all of the cases the social worker involved felt that the initiative had resulted in an improvement in the family's circumstances raises the possibility that the workers were inclined to re-assess the situation from an over-optimistic stance. After all they were working closely with the families, and in many of the cases had been involved in nominating the families for inclusion. As such, it could be argued, they had a vested interest in the scheme being judged a success. Such an association cannot be entirely disproved since the monitoring of the initiative depended in fact on the perceptions of the workers involved. However, the fact that only in two cases were the children received into care suggests that the generally positive comments of the social workers were justified.

It seems valid to conclude, then, that the initiative has been encouragingly successful in its principal objective of keeping united families who are at high risk of breakdown. As well as avoiding the need for reception into care, an overall improvement in the families' circumstances has been witnessed in most instances. In view of this it would appear that the Regional Council no longer needs to be so defensive in its approach to the use of Section 12 funding in this manner.

References

1. Social Work (Scotland) Act. HMSO, 1968.

2. Jackson, M. & Valencia, M. *Financial Aid Through Social Work*. Routledge & Kegan Paul, London, 1979.

3. Freeman, I. *Report on the Use of Section 12*. Strathclyde Regional Council, 1980.

4. Currie, H. & Davidson, R. *Social Workers, Clients and Financial Problems*. University of Edinburgh, 1982.

5. *Room to Grow*. Strathclyde Regional Council, 1979.

6. Wedge, P. & Essen, J. *Children in Adversity*. Pan, London, 1982.

7. Strathclyde Regional Council. *Analysis of Census and Population Data*. 1981.

8. *Burying Beveridge*. Child Poverty Action Group, London, 1985.

9. *Low Income Families*. Department of Health and Social Security, London, 1981.

10. Popay, J. *One Parent Families*. National Council for One Parent Families, London, 1983.

11. *Strathclyde Economic Trends*. Strathclyde Regional Council, June, 1984.

12. Strathclyde Regional Council. *Who Are They?* 1981, and see also McCluskey and Fegan in this volume.

13. Roberts, G., Reinach, E. & Lovelock, R. *Children on the Rates*. Social Services Research and Intelligence Unit, Portsmouth, 1976.

14. Report of the Committee on Children and Young Persons. Cmnd 1191, HMSO, London, 1960.

15. House of Commons. Second Report from the Social Services Committee Session 1983-84. *Children in Care*. 1, 1984.

16. Lishman, J. (Ed.) *Evaluation. 2nd edition. Research Highlights*, No.8, Jessica Kingsley, London, 1988.

Patterns, Policies and Issues in Child Care Reviews

Mel Cadman

INTRODUCTION

In this chapter the development of the review system within Strathclyde is described and the practice surrounding reviews is compared with available research data on practice elsewhere. Some of the limitations in Strathclyde's practice are then detailed and a brief description of the piloting of the new review procedures and how they can improve practice is provided.

Over the past few years the number of children physically in the Department's care at any one time has steadily decreased, even though the number being received into care has increased. Forty per cent of children received into care returned home to their parents within four weeks and 60% within six months.

These statistics differ from the trends described as existing at the time the DHSS-funded research reviewed in 'Decision Making in Child Care' was undertaken, when receptions into care were decreasing and the number in care static, and suggest the problem of 'drift' may not be as severe within Strathclyde as the DHSS report suggests is the case elsewhere [1]. The most obvious explanation for such a difference would appear to be in reviewing procedures, and comparison of the practice in Strathclyde with that revealed by research [2,3] as existing in England and Wales at the time of the DHSS studies would reinforce this view.

Despite this, within Strathclyde we are acutely aware of the inadequacies of our reviewing practice, and as a result the existing review procedures have recently been revamped, piloted in a number of area teams and are shortly to be introduced throughout the region.

The principle of developing a review system within the context of a coherent child care policy was first established in 1978 with the publication of 'Room to Grow', which was the product of an Officer-Member group whose responsibility was to define child care policy and practice within a unified philosophical framework [4].

It would be impossible to detail all of the influences which were brought to bear in the course of doing this, although clearly 'Born to Fail', The Houghton Committee Report, 'Children Who Wait', and 'Who Cares?' were some of the most influential sources [5,6,7,8]. The presence of elected councillors was intended to ensure that proposed changes to policy and practice were generally congruent with the prevailing political ethos of the Council. Although the scope of this report was very wide-ranging, the absence of a child care review system was a central concern that emerged frequently throughout all its sections. The reasons for proposing the creation of a child care review system were perhaps most succinctly stated in the following quote from the section entitled 'The Quality of Residential Care':

> '(A child care review system would) improve overall standards, introduce individual planning ... (and would obviate) the danger that children will languish without positive and specific plans for their future. Those who have any concern, interest or responsibility for the child should contribute ... Placement will be more effectively used, leading to more purposeful homes and improvement in the caring services ... A priority of any review system (should be) to identify children currently in residential care ... who would benefit from the opportunity of family life.'

The question of defining in detail how a review system should operate, and what part children and parents should play in the review process, was covered in the 'Social Policy for Children' section, thus:

> 'All children in the care of Strathclyde should have a case review at least every six months. The review should take the form of a *face to face meeting of all the key adults involved* and clear Regional operational guidelines should be formulated. It should be a *child's right to attend* his/her review and *participate as fully as possible. Reports and case papers should be available for the child to see ...*' (emphasis added).

The matter of parental involvement in reviews, clearly implied in the above, was emphasised elsewhere in the report.

The significance of creating a child care review system was, therefore, viewed as being to devise a process which positively helped: to improve general standards in child care, by monitoring; to ensure that purposeful and individual plans were made to ensure suitability of placement and avoiding 'drift' and equally, to give parents and children a definable right to involvement and active participation in the matter of monitoring practice and developing plans. To this end, the Officer-Member group defined the functions of the review as being a face-to-face meeting of all those with a legitimate concern for the child's life in care, such as social workers, carers, parents and children working jointly, and, if possible, in harmony to define and promote the child's best interests. If one phrase could be used to describe the distinctive feature of this concept, then 'mutual accountability' might be the most apt.

The introduction of a review package in 1981, consisting of a policy note and review forms, was intended to translate this basic concept into practice.

STRATHCLYDE'S REVIEWING PRACTICE: A COMPARISON WITH ITS OWN OBJECTIVES AND WITH THOSE OF OTHER AUTHORITIES

Establishing criteria by which to judge the effectiveness or otherwise of reviewing practice is a complex matter, depending upon interpretation and perceptions. Establishing comparative criteria is made even more difficult by virtue of the fact that the available literature makes many references to child care reviews but produces little work where a direct comparison with Strathclyde can easily be made. Any attempt to do this involves the selective inclusion of some issues and the exclusion of other issues which may be of equal or greater importance.

In acknowledgement of this, therefore, the following issues were selected because they appear to be capable of some comparative analysis:

> Who has responsibility for organising and chairing reviews; Who is invited to attend reviews; How many people attend reviews; What part do children and parents play in reviews; How long do reviews last; Who is asked to make written contributions; How involved are parents and children in their reviews; How well do they fulfil their decision-making function?

Since 1981 and the introduction of the review package there have been some developments in practice. The bases for determining Strathclyde's present practice were: an analysis of new forms piloted in three selected parts of the Region in 1986; the results of a survey of Children's Homes within one Division in 1985/86; formal contact between senior management and representatives of the foster care consultative group and the Regional 'Who Cares?' group. Comparisons are made principally with: Sinclair's work, 'Decision Making in Statutory Reviews on Children in Care' [2]; McDonnell and Aldgate's research: 'Review Procedures for Children in Care' [9]; Stein and Ellis' paper: 'Gizza Say' [10]; and the Children's Legal Centre publication [11], while reference is also made to a number of other publications less centrally devoted to the question of child care reviews.

Organisation and Chairing

In relation to the question of who has responsibility for convening and chairing reviews in Strathclyde, practice varies across the Region. While the responsibility is located formally with District Managers, practice indicates that line supervisors to the child's social worker are usually charged with this responsibility. Sinclair notes that the practice in her authority differentiated between children in residential and other forms of care. While important criticisms can also be levelled against reviewing practice organised centrally by specialist staff in residential care cases in this authority, the relatively greater skill and objectivity of such staff appear to make these reviews more purposeful. Observations would have suggested that locating responsibility with staff with direct line management responsibility for the case appeared to increase the dangers that such reviews were regarded as routine social work centred events which routinely excluded children, parents and carers. However partiality and collusion are increased when main-line supervisors are given responsibility for monitoring the effectiveness of their own staff.

Attendance

Who attends reviews in Strathclyde was prescribed from the outset as being

> 'interested agencies ... parents (both actual and foster) and child involvement should take place in every review ... unless a chairperson is satisfied that their involvement could be detrimental to the welfare of the child.'

While there is no information available about practice in Strathclyde generally, an analysis of the minutes form used for a pilot of new forms in 1986 does provide some limited evidence.

The average (mode) attendance at review meetings was seven and this was not greatly affected by whether the child was in residential or foster care. These figures can be directly compared with Sinclair's research. In 93.5 per cent of cases, only two people attended reviews of children living in foster care. Where children lived in residential care, a mode of eight was in attendance. It is accepted that the differing numbers attending cases where children live in residential, as opposed to foster care, are attributable to the fact that residential workers are well represented in the former, the implications of the differences between Strathclyde and Sinclair's authority are clear. Strathclyde appears normally to 'involve other agencies as appropriate', while in Sinclair's authority other people are almost universally excluded from foster placement reviews.

Who attends reviews is of more significance than the numbers, of course, and again some evidence is available from the pilot exercise. First, carers. Carers, whether residential social workers or foster parents, attended in 98 per cent of cases, a figure clearly confirming their attendance to be the norm. Given the importance of the contribution which they can make to reviews, it is surprising to note that Sinclair's authority invited foster parents to attend in only one out of 292 cases observed, although the presence of residential social workers was normal in residential reviews.

What other evidence is available? McDonnell and Aldgate [9], who surveyed all authorities in England in 1984, confirmed that it is frequent practice to exclude foster parents from reviews; only 25 per cent of authorities indicated that it was their normal practice to invite them. And while more than 74 per cent of such authorities invited residential social workers to attend reviews, their observations about the effect of regular exclusion of carers seems appropriate:

> 'Only if a full review meeting takes place ... will there be an opportunity to challenge social workers' assertions ... and provide alternative views ... Given that at times the social worker is not the key person in a child's life ... a standard practice in many agencies of leaving the task of reporting on progress in one pair of hands should be questioned.'

Participation of Children and Parents

This concern is also appropriately directed to the issue of parents, and children's, attendance at reviews. The pilot exercise of 1986 showed that 80 per cent of children were present at reviews, rising to 86 per cent where the factor of being over 12 years of age is taken into account, comparing favourably with the figures of 0 per cent (for foster placements) and 9.8 per cent (for residential placements) in Sinclair's authority. McDonnell and Aldgate's research indicates that the pattern of attendance of children at reviews is generally better, although nowhere as common as in Strathclyde.

However, the question of parental attendance at reviews in Strathclyde is less reassuring. In the cases analysed, parents attended in only 24 per cent of reviews, in stark contrast with the stated policy. As there was no means of determining what the reasons were for parents' non-attendance at reviews, a cross tabulation of the placement objectives by their attendance was computed in the expectation that their exclusion was justified by their having no effective parental role to fulfil. The results of this computation were that in cases where rehabilitation was planned, parental attendance increased to 70 per cent of cases. If, however, it is accepted in cases where permanence may be assumed to be the objective of placement, the low level of parental attendance (less than 10 per cent) must call into question whether a residual but important role, such as containing some form of contact with the child, could ever have been addressed in a number of cases where it was appropriate. Unfortunately the imprecise recording of parental access during this pilot exercise did not make it possible to determine whether parental exclusion and nominally continuing access went hand in hand.

The comparison between Strathclyde and other authorities reported in the literature does, however, show the comparative position to be reasonably good. Thus, in Sinclair's research, parental attendance was almost non-existent, while McDonnell and Aldgate's research concluded that 75 per cent of authorities included parents only 'occasionally'. Nevertheless, their exclusion from so many reviews in Strathclyde increases the dangers referred to in McDonnell and Aldgate's paper, that

> 'There is real danger that the social worker can stand in judgement of clients ... while providing no opportunity for them to comment on the fairness of the judgement.'

Attendance does not, of course, guarantee involvement in reviews, and the process of determining whether involvement takes place is a necessarily complex one. Again, it is necessary selectively to establish comparative criteria which can be held to promote involvement, and it is argued that the following factors give some simple indication of how it is best achieved.

Duration of Meetings

The first of these is the length of review meetings. Sinclair states that

> 'The length of time a review lasts presumably does say something about what the participants hope to gain from a review and therefore how they perceive the purpose and importance of the review.'

If it is accepted that, within limits, the longer a review meeting lasts the more probable it is that it will create an opportunity to consider various contributions, Strathclyde's practice would appear to be reasonably sound. While there is no objective evidence available to support this, seasoned practitioners and managers within the authority have judged that the 'normal' review lasts between three-quarters and one and a quarter hours, depending on the complexity of the case. Sinclair's research indicates that her authority had reviews which lasted ten minutes or less in 51.9 per cent of foster placements reviewed, whereas reviews within residential units lasted between half and one hour in 61 per cent of cases.

Written Submissions

Who is asked to make written contributions to reviews also makes for interesting comparisons. In the case of Strathclyde, foster parents and residential care workers are always asked to make a written contribution and the pilot exercise confirmed that this is nearly always achieved. McDonnell and Aldgate found that in only 40 per cent of authorities were residential social workers asked to report to reviews and that this percentage declined to only 20 per cent with regard to foster parents. In this respect, then, Strathclyde appears much more regularly to use written contributions from carers, thereby minimising the opportunities for social workers alone to influence decisions.

Inviting parents and children to make written contributions to reviews appears to be exceptional, despite the evidence available from Stein and Ellis [10], the Children's Legal Centre [11] and others, that this practice can be instrumental in engaging the attention and active involvement of both at review meetings. In only four out of the 78 authorities surveyed by McDonnell and Aldgate, were such written contributions requested, and in Sinclair's authority there was no evidence that it ever happened. It is puzzling to understand on what basis such exclusions are justified. Certainly, in Strathclyde, the absence of review forms for parents and children is compounded by the relative infrequency where the views of either are sought explicitly in either the social worker's or carer's forms and this appears to be commonplace elsewhere. Even if these forms were designed in such a way as clearly to elicit the views of children and parents, evidence from Gersch and Cutting [12] has suggested that children's perceptions of their life in care may be quite different from those with responsibility for them, even if they work in close proximity to them. Other evidence, available from the survey of Children's Homes, undertaken in Strathclyde in 1986, and from a study of young people leaving care, the fieldwork for which was largely undertaken in Strathclyde [13], also testifies to the sense of exclusion which such children experienced, even where they actually attended reviews.

The Perceptions of Children and Parents

The question of how children and parents perceive care and, in particular, the process of reviews, was one which was considered in the course of surveying Children's Homes, within one Division of Strathclyde. The findings in relation to children identified a number of concerns which were common-place. The first concern was that of how ill-prepared they were for review meetings. Many indicated that they had not been shown the reports to be used at meetings before the meeting took place, some indicating that they were not given access to the report even at the meeting and that the language used in reports and during the meetings was equally confusing and incomprehensible to them. The few who had had the opportunity to use a report form for their own reviews found this a useful and stimulating way in which to prompt discussion about issues of central importance to them. The survey concluded that the criticisms voiced by children were generally valid and that the introduction of report forms, combined with the careful chairing of meetings, could do much to remedy these avoidable defects.

In relation to the question of parents' perception of child care reviews, the findings from our consultation with parents were very similar. Many did not appear to appreciate the importance of review meetings, some were ill-equipped to follow the discussion and a general sense of cynicism prevailed that the meetings were designed simply to rubber-stamp the views of social workers and their managers. It was also concluded that the introduction of a form for parents would do much to enhance their sense of participation at meetings.

Comparisons with practice elsewhere are surprisingly difficult to make because of the scarcity of research, particularly in relation to parents, although children's perceptions of reviews were well illustrated in Stein and Ellis' paper 'Gizza Say'. This indicates the general applicability of these complaints, among a more diffuse population of children in care, but, like the survey already referred to, illustrates the possibility of constructing review systems and aids in such a way as to increase the meaningful participation of children at reviews. There is no reason to presume that similar remedies would not do as much to help parents make equally meaningful contributions to reviews.

Decision-Making

The final, and perhaps most important issue about reviewing practice, must be the extent to which it effectively monitors practice and formulates realistic and precise decisions. It is important that reviews are used to effectively monitor practice, and recording procedures should allow analysis of the type undertaken by Sinclair in her research to be a regular part of the review system. The new review system which will be linked to the department's computerised child care information system should ensure that in future this will be the case.

Does practice measure up to the objectives of the review policy? The earlier instruction in the review document of 1981 made it clear that review meetings should be held at 'appropriate intervals', presumably in an attempt to ensure that reviews were the focal point of decision-making where children were in care. This flexibility does not appear to have happened if the development of the child care strategies within the department and the associated memos which accompany them are to be construed as a reasoned response to actual practice. Thus, for example, instructions have had to be issued that the decision to pursue parental rights should be taken only at reviews and that plans for rehabilitation should be dealt with similarly. Instructions have also had to be issued to ensure that changes to placement are, where possible, preceded by review meetings, or are at least confirmed by them shortly afterwards.

There is also some evidence that decisions made to assume parental rights, for example, are not associated with establishing an appropriate time-scale in which to complete this process. It would appear, therefore, that the underlying principle of making reviews conform to the needs of the case, rather than vice-versa, has not been well served in practice. Fisher et al. have noted the prevalence of this problem elsewhere when they stated that

> 'Care sometimes developed into an end in itself with little sense of purpose or plan [14].'

Sinclair also observed from her authority that

> 'Although reviews played a part in the making of major decisions, this was not a dominant part.'

Strathclyde would seem to share in many of the difficulties evident elsewhere, although it has at least provided a framework in which the review mechanism can meet the needs of its children in care.

The dual questions posed: How does Strathclyde's review policy and practice meet its stated objectives and how does it compare with other authorities, are not easy to answer. In terms of judging how effectively policy and practice meets the objectives stated in 'Room to Grow', there are successes and failures. On the positive side, policy and practice appear to have secured a regular review system which normally involves social workers and carers, children and parents, in the 'face-to-face' meetings initially envisaged as the review process. Bit by bit it appears to have made progress towards ensuring that review meetings are a focal point for making crucial decisions about children in care. However, it has failed by and large to produce review forms which are as relevant and meaningful to those that use them as they could be. Parents and children, in particular, have not been helped to make better use of the review system for reasons which could have been remedied very simply. It is a moot question whether reviewing practice achieves its most important task of monitoring and planning.

Comparison with practice elsewhere confirms the existence of common problems, particularly in relation to the meaningful involvement of children and parents, and that of ensuring that the reviews fulfil their monitoring and planning functions. However, it also demonstrates clearly that carers, children and parents are provided with the means to voice opinions in a way which makes it unusually, if not uniquely, progressive. If the aim of securing active participation requires some fundamental re-appraisal in Strathclyde at least it has achieved a sound bedrock on which to build.

A NEW REVIEW PACKAGE

It has been argued that while Strathclyde succeeded in realising some of the most important features of good practice, such as a regular review system, child, and to a lesser extent parental involvement in the review process, in marked contrast with the practice of reviewing surveyed in the literature, significant shortcomings were also evident. These comprised basic design faults in the policy document and the forms, together with the failure to recognise the essential role which chairing of meetings would play in maximising its potential. Of equal significance were the difficulties encountered in implementation because of inadequate staffing levels, lack of training for staff and foster parents and lack of clarity in defining the central role of District Managers.

The development of child care practice generally, reflected in the creation of the child care strategy papers within Strathclyde [15] and the introduction of Phase III of the Children Act, 1975 [16] and HASSASSA, 1984 [17], compounded the problems to such an extent that a radical re-appraisal of the whole review package was required by 1984. This reappraisal has now been completed but the new package has not yet been introduced.

The creation of this new package, consisting of both the review policy document and the forms to be used at the reviews, was undertaken only after careful scrutiny of the available literature, particularly Sinclair [2], McDonnell and Aldgate [9], so that the two components would match the best possible standards of review practice. Equally, the origins of the review concept were closely scrutinised to ensure that the basic philosophical framework of 'Room to Grow' was enhanced. Taken together this suggested that the central themes to be addressed in devising any package were: improving the quantity and quality of information conveyed to reviews; promoting the active participation of parents and children; providing a more rigorous system to facilitate decision-making at reviews; increasing the impartiality, objectivity and professionalism of chairing reviews; defining the central role of senior management in a specific way and introducing an appeal mechanism.

The culmination of this re-appraisal was twofold. In the first place the new review policy makes radical changes to the way in which child care reviews should be organised, structured and conducted. Of the many detailed changes which this brought about, perhaps the most innovative was that of establishing the principle of having a Core Group at all reviews. In effect, this created a quorum for a review meeting, in which the rights and responsibilities of not only parents, children, carers and social workers to attend reviews were established, but also those with a direct supervisory or supportive responsibility for placement. The underlying intention is to create a process of mutual accountability in which both providers and recipients of the service jointly define and work towards establishing agreed placement objectives.

The new system also clearly places the responsibility for ensuring decisions are taken and monitoring the implementation of these decisions with district management. In addition it has been made clear in Strathclyde that certain types of decision, for example, the decision to apply for parental rights, can only be taken at a review. This approach differs from that adopted by a number of other authorities, for example, Lothian. Finally, the new system has ensured that certain issues, most importantly access arrangements, are addressed at each review.

The tools to achieve the objectives of promoting good practice are the new child care review forms. The complete package of review forms has been substantially revised to take into account the implications of the new review policy and also to incorporate the lessons from practice both within and outwith Strathclyde. To that end, the following objectives were the ones which were agreed to be of most importance, thus: to depict a comprehensive, dynamic and balanced picture of the child and, where appropriate, natural parents; to record in an analytical and constructive way issues about contact between a child and his natural family, including siblings, other relatives, etc.; to reach conclusions based on evidence and reasoned interpretation; actively to seek specific proposals for the child's future based on conclusions reached; to facilitate and identify children's and parents' perceptions and future proposals; carefully to examine the implications for placement of any proposals made. Forms were designed to further these objectives and were piloted within three Districts of the Region, exhaustively debated with users and analysed objectively by a representative group, with the help of a computer. The results of this piloting exercise have been used to produce a series of forms which will be introduced, along with the new review policy, in the near future.

Implications of the Pilot Exercise

The by-product of undertaking a pilot of the new review forms as well as giving us a picture of present practice was also to highlight a number of practice issues of some considerable importance. There were clearly difficulties in recording discussion. Placement objectives and social work support were often completely missed or vaguely recorded in the relevant new sections, although the narrative account would often indicate that these matters had been actually discussed at the meeting. What was much more important, however, was the fact that in a substantial number of cases parental arrangements had not been specified (in any parts of the form) and parental dissent had been recorded so rarely that it was statistically insignificant. Given the number and wide range of cases, it is difficult to believe that dissent occurred so rarely; however the conclusion had to be drawn that it was either not acknowledged as such, or that, if it were, a decision was made not to record it. Examination of the narrative part of the minutes report indicated, furthermore, that parental and children's views of any type were rarely recorded. Similarly, there was little evidence in the appropriate section, or even in the narrative account, that the question of information and resources, for either carers or parents, had been discussed at all.

The Region's commitment to intensive training around the issue of parental access might have been expected to create a general awareness that this was one of the principal functions of reviews. While a cross-tabulation of access arrangements by age of child does demonstrate that the responsibilities were fulfilled much more regularly in cases where young children under 12 were in care, the number of other occasions when it was simply ignored shows a disregard for both Regional policy and statutory requirement.

Although one should be cautious of making generalisations, which may be attributable to relative inexperience in using a new minutes form, the overall picture from the objective analysis of completed minutes would suggest that the current standard of chairing and recording review meetings in the Region leaves much to be desired. Reviews appeared to be occasions when issues for discussion were selected because they seemed to be immediately relevant rather than to be an opportunity systematically and rigorously to examine the purposes of placement in terms of the child's complete development. Thus, current issues and problems appeared to pre-occupy the discussion to a considerable extent, while the child's past history, and complete personality development, particularly in the areas of progress, seemed to be largely ignored. Illustrations of this are: the general failure to record whether parental access has some role to play, whether some current difficulty might be attributable to past causes and whether current placement was as suitable to the child as it could be. The conclusions reached, therefore, were that the basic concept of this type of minutes form was an acceptable means of recording decisions made at reviews, if not the only means possible, and that its ability to highlight practice issues about chairing and recording review meetings so effectively, made it an ideal tool for monitoring and analysing practice.

A major dilemma was posed by the poor response of many foster parents, particularly long-term foster parents and foster parents related to the child, to the new forms especially in relation to the narrative part of the form.

Foster parents, if they can usefully be described as a discrete group, appear to experience bewilderingly different systems for training, support and supervision, depending on where they live, how their function is defined and who they experience as their social worker. If they happen to work as 'temporary' or 'contract' foster parents and are assigned to a centralised team, they appear to be confident in describing themselves as professionals, working towards defined placement objectives in harmony with children, parents and social workers, thereby willingly accepting the task of recording, analysing and offering observations on key issues to the child. This relatively small group of foster parents is well placed to take its part in the review process in the way which the review policy document and associated forms implies.

With the other, more amorphous group of foster parents consisting in the main of relatives to the child and other long-term foster parents, little training, support or supervision is effectively offered. Their role definition tends to sit uneasily with that of working towards defined placement objectives with children, parents and social workers, such that the process of recording, etc., seems to be rather alien to them. Given these factors, it is not surprising that the new review package, but particularly the new forms, have encountered marked resistance.

Strathclyde has a major job of work to do if it is to ensure that both, but particularly the latter group of foster parents, are enabled to take an effective part in maximising the potential of the new review package. Certainly the organisation of training could play an important part in helping this process along but, equally, the matter of ongoing support to foster parents has to be quickly addressed [18].

Another dominant practice theme was that of the part played by social workers and carers in preparing children and parents for review meetings, an issue which simply cannot be ignored if they are to be helped to make best use of the more complex structure and function of review meetings in future. The evidence from piloting would suggest that there is considerable willingness to undertake or refine the approach to this task, but again the implications for effective deployment of scarce staff resources is not inconsiderable.

Unfortunately, the most innovative aspect of the review package was one which could not be introduced to the piloting exercise because of trades union opposition. Where occasional use was made of either or both forms, there was general acclaim that the parents' and child's forms offered new insights, new information and established dialogue in a way which made a major impact upon child care reviews. It is to be hoped that negotiations will continue to take place so that these forms can be introduced at the same time as the rest of the package.

Strathclyde believes that it has now developed and designed a review system which can fulfil all the expectations generated by 'Room to Grow' and which can meet developing practice standards, for some time in the future. What it must also do, however, is to learn from its mistakes in the past, by ensuring that all staff and foster parents are brought to the point where they can fully appreciate the purposes and benefits of the new system. No system of this sort can hope to realise anything like its full potential unless the individuals involved in the process can knowledgeably, and willingly participate. If Strathclyde were able to achieve this, child care decision-making could improve immeasurably.

References

1. DHSS. *Social Work Decisions in Child Care: Recent Research Findings and their Implications.* HMSO, London, 1985.

2. Sinclair, R. *Decision Making in Statutory Reviews on Children in Care.* Gower, 1984.

3. Vernon, J. & Fruin, D. *In Care.* National Children's Bureau, London, 1986.

4. Strathclyde Regional Council. Officer Member Group Report. *Room to Grow.* 1978.

5. Wedge, P. and Prosser, H. *Born to Fail?* Arrow Books, London, 1973.

6. Houghton Committee (1972). *Report of the Departmental Committee on the Adoption of Children.* Cmnd. 5107, HMSO.

7. Rowe, J. & Lambert, L. *Children Who Wait.* Association of British Adoption Agencies, London, 1973.

8. Page, R. & Clark, G.A. *Who Cares? Young People in Care Speak Out.* National Children's Bureau, London, 1977.

9. McDonnell, P., Aldgate, J. 'Research: Review Procedures for Children in Care' *Adoption and Fostering.* 18, 3, 1984.

10. Stein, M. & Ellis, S. *Gizza Say.* National Association of Young People in Care, 1983.

11. Children's Legal Centre. *The Need for a Change.* London, 1983.

12. Gersch, I., Cutting, M.L. 'A Child's Eye View' *Community Care.* 24.01.85.

13. Morgan Klein, B. *Where am I Going to Stay?* Scottish Council for Single Homeless, Edinburgh, 1985.

14. Fisher, M., Marsh, P., Phillip, D. with Sainsbury, F. *In and Out of Care.* Batsford, London, 1986.

15. See Freeman, Montgomery & Moore in this volume.

16. The Children Act, HMSO, 1975.

17. Health and Social Services and Social Security Adjudications Act. Chapter 41. HMSO, 1983.

18. See Freeman in this volume.

Development of Child Abuse Practice in Strathclyde Region

Bernadette Docherty, Colin Findlay and Fraser McCluskey

INTRODUCTION

This chapter considers the development of Strathclyde's response to child abuse, drawing from the department's information system and from a study of the children on the child abuse register in 1980. It goes on to look at some of the problems facing workers in the child abuse field at present and stresses the need for training and support.

As is the case in most authorities in the United Kingdom, Strathclyde has become increasingly involved in the last 15 years or so with the rising public and media concern surrounding child abuse. From the Maria Colwell case in 1973 [1] to the Cleveland enquiry in 1987 [2], the publicity and controversy surrounding social work child abuse monitoring and practice has resulted in continual cries for change. Not surprisingly, there has been a growing volume of literature on the subject from academics and practitioners, advocating various reforms and reflecting the very real anxieties being experienced by professionals working in the field. This chapter concentrates on the development of practice in Strathclyde but developments in many other authorities will have been similar.

Child care practice in the latter half of the 1970s was greatly affected by the Children Act 1975 [3] which was being implemented in a piecemeal fashion over this period and in the early 1980s. This Act, which was produced after the deliberations of the Houghton Committee [4], gave a new direction to legislation covering children. It moved away from seeing children as the property of their parents to emphasising the need to ensure that decisions made about children are governed by consideration of their needs and interests. Section 83 of the Children Act inserted in Section 37 of the Social Work (Scotland) Act stated:

> 'Where a Local Authority receives information suggesting that a child may
> be in need of compulsory measures of care, they shall (a) cause enquiries to

be made into the case unless they are satisfied that such enquiries are unnecessary and (b) if it appears to them that the child be in need of compulsory measures of care, give to the Reporter such information about the child as they may have been able to discover' [5].

The effect of this sub-section is to make it mandatory to investigate referrals of alleged ill treatment of children.

The Development of Procedures

Following the death of Maria Colwell in 1973 and later child abuse enquiries, the Social Work Services Group [6] highlighted strategies and procedures for handling situations of child abuse and advocating the setting up of local Child Abuse Registers and inter-agency case conferences. By 1980 each of the five Divisions in Strathclyde had its own set of procedures to facilitate workers identifying children who had been abused, to promote the effect of co-ordination with other agencies, to assess the needs of children and their families and to provide appropriate services. They also covered the maintenance of a Register of all children who had suffered from abuse or who were considered to be 'at risk' of abuse. A major feature of these Divisional Procedures was the establishment of Case Conferences as outlined by the Government Circular of 1975 [6]. It stated that

> 'a case conference is recommended for every case involving suspected non-accidental injury to a child. In this way, unilateral action would be minimized and all those who could provide information about the child and his family, who had a statutory responsibility for the safety of the child or were responsible for providing services, would be brought together to reach a collective decision taking into account the age of the child, the nature of the injuries and a medical/social assessment of the family and its circumstances.' [6]

Child Abuse in Strathclyde in 1980

In 1980 following the death of a child who had been placed on the department's child abuse register [7] a review of the department's practice was undertaken. Social workers were asked to complete a questionnaire providing detailed information on each child on the register in June 1980. At that time there were 719 cases on the register. The results of the analysis of this data allowed for the first time a description of how child abuse was perceived in Strathclyde to be presented [8]. Gough, Boddy, Dunning and Stone stress, 'the concept (of child abuse) is dependent not only upon the presenting features of a child and his/her environment, but upon the interpretations and reactions to these circumstances' [9].

Our study of the register raised a number of important issues, although it must be stressed that this information and the more recent analysis of our data discussed below does not tell us about all child abuse but only child abuse as it is experienced by workers in the social work department of Strathclyde. As Gough et al. point out, most samples studied are affected by this filter and yet often the effect of this bias is little appreciated.

The 1980 study found there was an even split between the number of male and female children on the register, eight per cent were aged under one and around a half were aged four or more. Prior to this study it had not been realised just how inappropriate the perception of child abuse as 'baby battering' was to Strathclyde.

Previous studies [10,11,12,13,14] had identified prematurity, the existence of abnormal medical features at birth and early separation from the mother as being associated with abuse. Social workers were asked about the existence of these factors, but these were not found to be significant. This may have been because social workers did not know of their existence rather than because they did not exist, but in any case it was clear that social workers did not find them to be pertinent in their approach to the case.

In 53 per cent of cases the male carer was the natural parent, in 10 per cent a stepfather, in 14 per cent a cohabitee, in 4 per cent some other male relative such as grandfather or uncle, and in 19 per cent of cases there was no male carer. Alcohol problems were a factor in 75 per cent of the cases, crime in 60 per cent, family violence in 40 per cent and mental illness in 20 per cent. A study of cases in England and Wales carried out by Creighton slightly earlier had found alcohol and crime to be much less significant [15], but other studies have noted a correlation although alcohol is not necessarily seen as a causative factor [16,17]. Looking at the inter-relationship of these problems in the Strathclyde data two patterns of Non Accidental Injury were identified.

'The more common is NAI in families where alcohol problems, violent behaviour and violent crime are present, often associated with the father figure being out of work and with his being a stepfather or cohabitee. The other pattern is NAI from single parent mothers who have recently moved house and, under strain may be showing signs of mental illness' [8].

When the registration criteria were considered it was found that almost a quarter of the cases were registered for precautionary reasons in many cases because they had a brother or sister who had been assaulted. In a quarter of cases non-physical injury was the criterion for registration, and in a quarter of cases bruising was identified. In only 24 per cent of cases were injuries such as cuts, burns and fractures referred to and sexual abuse was rarely mentioned. In 45 per cent of the cases which were registered for non-precautionary reasons the perpetrator was identified. In 37 per cent of these cases the natural mother was identified as the perpetrator, and in 32 per cent the natural father. The view that most child abuse was caused by male cohabitees was disproved. However it must be acknowledged that in 38 per cent of cases where a male cohabitee was present, he was believed to be the perpetrator.

Gough et al. argued in their review of child abuse research that

> 'Most of the data on total population of identified cases is collected by the agencies who have been making the identifications. An obvious and also less problematic use of the prevalence and "features" research would be to provide management information to these agencies. Unfortunately, much of the raw data reflects a "nature of child abuse" approach rather than describing how the cases fit into the agencies' often well developed systems of management. This is most obviously seen by the paucity of data describing the type and length of service offered to children on the Child Abuse Register or the eventual outcome in terms of placement of the child' [9].

Our study in 1980 looked at the Department's response.

A clear indication of the need for a procedural review was the extent of variation in practice identified. The rate of registration in districts varied by a ratio of 10 to 1 and although this can partly be explained by the different levels of deprivation in these areas (areas scoring highly on deprivation indicators were found to have high rates of NAI registration) this could not account for all the variation. The average time spent on the register was 16 and a half months but this too varied between districts. A tendency for cases where non physical injuries were identified to be on the register for longer was also evident.

The source of referral varied but in 15 per cent it was the parent and this, coupled with the fact that in two-thirds of the cases the child remains at home, suggests that such cases required workers to work with the family as a whole rather than remove the child [8]. The study carried out by Gough et al. made similar comments [9]. On average social workers spent 3.2 hours per week on such cases but most would have liked to have spent longer.

Day nurseries and homemakers were being used to provide support in a number of cases, but the need for more resources of this type was frequently commented on. Finally social workers were also found to be concerned about the lack of training they received, particularly on pre-qualifying courses, and a demand for in-service training was identified. Support from colleagues was valued but support from senior management at that time was felt to be lacking.

Regional Procedures

This report was published in August 1982 and by 1983 the five sets of Divisional Procedures Manuals had been reviewed and incorporated into one Regional Manual [18]. The danger of the Manual having a negative rather than a positive impact was recognised by the Department and the preface to these indicated

> 'that clear procedures (may) mitigate against good practice; that they add to a level of anxiety which staff already feel towards many tasks in Social Work; that staff come to set a higher priority upon obedience to the procedures than to the provision of a good sensitive service in the particular case, with all its special circumstances and considerations.'

Despite this, it was felt that the procedures would be a helpful tool in guiding staff through organisational expectations in relation to this field of work and the idea of shared responsibility between individual members of staff directly concerned with a family, and other staff throughout the Department, did seem to be seen as supportive and helpful. The procedures identified a need for the department to assume the central role in all child abuse cases. The department therefore had to ensure it was equipped to take on this role. It was agreed that the procedures

> 'constitute norms of practice, agreed by the Social Work Committee for staff working with children who are being, may have been, or are at risk of being victims of child abuse.'

With the publication of the Department's Procedures, in 1983 a massive training programme was implemented for all staff who would be involved with child abuse cases – only qualified social workers were to be used in these circumstances. Although the training course successfully ensured that workers were familiar with the legislation and indicators of abuse, staff still found it difficult to work with families who were abusing their children. Some staff felt ill-equipped to deal with issues relating to child abuse, and felt burdened by the high expectations of the Department and there was a growing awareness of the clear limitations of social work training to equip people to deal competently with the task.

Particular concerns were

(1) the difficulty of defining child abuse which results from the lack of knowledge about society's normal child rearing practices

(2) fear that procedural expectations would result in the priority in decision making becoming the safeguarding of the worker and the organisation rather than the child

(3) the feeling that the criteria used for registering children varied depending on the case conference chairman

(4) concern that despite the fact that all parents were informed of their child's registration, their participation at case conference reviews still varied.

Issues pertaining to the civil liberties of families and the family's right to manage its own affairs continue to conflict with society's responsibility to safeguard its most vulnerable members. Media focus in the past has usually centred on the failure of social workers in child abuse cases to safeguard the child although more recently stress has been placed on the rights of the parents. These problems remain.

The child abuse procedures are at present under review and despite the concerns identified above they appear to have withstood the test of time. In preparation for the review all area offices were contacted and asked for their views on the existing procedures. Their response was overwhelmingly positive.

Types of Abuse

Table 1 shows the category under which the child is registered.

TABLE 1

Abuse category	1987	%
Physical injury	294	31
Sex abuse	129	14
Physical neglect	51	5
Failure to thrive	8	1
Child at risk	468	49
Total	950	100

Recent Trends in Child Abuse

During the period following the 1983 procedures there was a reduction in the number of children placed on the register and by April 1985 there were only 655 cases registered. However, in common with many other authorities following the media publicity regarding the deaths of children in several social services departments and child sexual abuse, Strathclyde has experienced an increase in both referrals and registrations [19,20]. In March 1987 the number of children on the child abuse register was 950. Ranked with other Scottish authorities Strathclyde's rate of registration per 1000 of the child population lies somewhere in the middle [20].

Defining clearly situations which should be seen as involving abuse is difficult [9]. Recent guidelines make the criteria for registration under the above categories, and how Strathclyde's criteria relate to government guidelines, clear.

Physical Injury. The SWSG circular SW4/84 [21] explains this as:

> 'All physically injured children under the age of 16 years where the nature of the injury is not consistent with the account of how it occurred; and/or where there is definite knowledge, or a reasonable suspicion, that the injury was inflicted (or knowingly not prevented) by any person having custody, charge, or care of the child. This includes children to whom it is suspected poisonous substances have been administered. Diagnosis of child abuse will normally require both medical examination of the child and social assessment of the family background.'

This category covers all seriously injured children. It covers broken limbs, fractures, cuts or lacerations, head injuries, internal injuries, suffocation, burns and poisoning. It should also cover bruising, and the guidelines suggest that if the concern about child abuse is sufficient to lead to a recommendation of registration, then this category must be used no matter how minor the injury.

Sexual Abuse of Children. The SWSG circular excluded sexual abuse as a separate category for registration. The concern about the effects of sexual abuse of children was such that in 1983 Strathclyde Social Work Department introduced the operation of a sub-category of physical injury (PI(S)) which covered all serious forms of sexual abuse. This included all forms of sexual abuse involving physical contact, irrespective of injury. With the introduction of this sub-section it had been agreed that non-physical sexual abuse (exposing a child to witness intercourse, or pornographic material) should also be registered under the new sub-category. This was monitored regionally since the introduction of this sub-section, and as the total within this section now represents 14 per cent of all registrations it has now been decided that physical injury (sexual) should be a category of registration in its own right.

Physical Neglect. The Social Work Services Group circular explains this as 'children under the age of 16 years who have been persistently or severely neglected physically.' The draft circular of 1981 gave it as an example 'by exposure to dangers of different kinds, including cold and starvation.' This may involve one incident of *severe* physical neglect (e.g. being out overnight in freezing conditions) or a series of incidents of less severe neglect – a *persistent* failure to adequately feed or clothe or *persistent* exposure to hazards or *persistent* pattern of being left unattended.

Failure to Thrive. The SWSG circular explains this as 'children under the age of 16 who have been medically diagnosed as suffering from severe non-organic failure to thrive, where it is suspected this may be due to neglect.'

This is the most difficult category to define. The essence of this category is that there is a physical effect measurable, medical or psychologically, e.g. by height – weight – age tables for age development. This effect may be due to emotional or mental abuse as well as neglect. Emotional abuse, however, defined in itself is not a ground for registration if it does not have an outcome of severe failure to thrive.

The essential elements of this category are:

(a) A medical assessment of severe failure to thrive.
(b) A medical diagnosis that this failure is non-organic.
(c) A social assessment that this failure is due to neglect, rejection or emotional abuse.

Children at Risk. The SWSG circular explains this as:

> 'children under the age of 16 who are considered to be at risk of abuse or are in a household with another person who has abused a child or with another child who has been abused and are *themselves* considered at risk of abuse.'

This category is the cause of most of the variations in registration. The obvious question, often not adequately answered in the 49 per cent of cases currently on the register is 'at risk of what?'.

The SWSG circular makes it clear that being in a household with a person who has abused a child, or with another child who has been abused, is not in *itself* sufficient grounds for registration. They must also be themselves considered at risk of abuse. There should be grounds for this related to the child in question.

Physical neglect and failure to thrive as defined above either exist or not. It is not felt useful to have an active concept of at risk of either. '*At risk' then should be restricted to children at risk of physical injury and there should be clear grounds as to the nature of the risk for each child.*

Child Abuse in Strathclyde in 1987

As has been said, almost all authorities have been experiencing increases in the numbers on their child abuse register. Consideration of the trends in individual categories for registration within Strathclyde shows this increase is not a general one in all categories. The number of children placed on the register as a result of physical injuries excluding sexual abuse and non-physical injuries have actually decreased. The increase in the number of registrations is accounted for, therefore, by an increase in the numbers registered under the sexual abuse and at risk categories.

The 950 children on the Register come from a total of 544 households. Three hundred and eight children had no other member of the family on the Register, while 62 children who were registered had four or more siblings on the Register. On average, a ratio of 1:1.7 children were registered per household, and this is similar to the figures highlighted in the 1980 [9] report.

Those categorised at risk are often the siblings of children registered as a result of physical injury, including sexual abuse. The increase in the at risk category therefore may be explained in part by the increasing identification of sexual abuse, but there also appears to be a tendency to use the 'at risk' category in cases where abuse of the child or any siblings has not been unquestionably established. This increase may be the result of the increased professional anxiety brought about by recent media publicity [20].

In terms of gender, girls outnumber boys 3:1 in sexual abuse cases compared to a 50:50 ratio over the Register as a whole. Of the 114 girls aged 12-15 approximately 50 per cent are on the Register because of sexual abuse problems. The consequent increase in demands on already stretched social work agencies has been well documented in the media publicity surrounding the Cleveland enquiry [2].

Table 2 shows the age sex breakdown of those children on the Register. Two-thirds of the children are aged eight or under, while just over 20 per cent are aged 12.

TABLE 2

Age	M	F	Total	%
0–4	212	195	407	43
5–8	126	87	213	23
9–11	63	62	125	13
12–15	68	114	182	19
16–17	11	12	23	2
Total	480	470	950	100

Comparison with the 1980 study shows an increase in the proportion of children aged 12 or more on the register. The 1980 Report found that those aged 12 made up only 7 per cent of the total. The increase is clearly the result of the increasing awareness of the physical and sexual abuse of young women aged 12 and over.

Examination of initial referral source shows large variations across the Region and this reflects the varying activities of agencies and the varying quality of the relationship between social work and these agencies. On average, health-related personnel refer 13 per cent of cases, schools 14 per cent, neighbours and friends 10 per cent, and police 10 per cent. The number of referrals from anonymous callers shows a significant rise since 1980. An increasing proportion are also picked up at evenings and weekends by the Region's Emergency Services.

The findings on family background are broadly similar to those in the 1980 study. In 55 per cent of cases the natural mother and father lived together, a figure which is higher than the proportion of natural parents living together for all admissions to care (30 per cent). The proportion of cases where there was no male carer has increased, however, from 19 to 26 per cent.

Where a physical injury took place and the perpetrator was known, in 45 per cent of cases it was the natural father, in 25 per cent it was the natural mother, and in 16 per cent it was another male carer. In a further 7 per cent it was a related adult and in 5 per cent a non-related adult. This again dispels some myths commonly held by the media and public about the non-blood connections being more guilty of abusing children. The decrease in the proportion of natural mothers identified as perpetrators may partly reflect the increasing number of sexual abuse cases.

Length of Time on Register

Early analysis of the length of time children spend on the Register shows that approximately 40 per cent at any one point in time have been on the Register for less than six months. Thirty one per cent have been on for between six and 12 months, and over ten per cent have been on for over two years. The percentages vary dramatically across Districts and different local authorities, reflecting once more the various professional attitudes towards child abuse supervision [20]. Recent indications show that children in Strathclyde are remaining longer on Registers than previously, thereby contributing to the increase in the numbers of children on the Register, and further investigation of this issue is under way.

TABLE 3

Accommodation type of child at time of registration

	No.	%
At home	565	59
Non-related fostering	143	15
LA children's home	91	10
With relatives not fostered	59	6
Hospital	38	4
Other	54	6
Total	950	100

Approximately 60 per cent of children were staying at home at the time of registration. This represents a slight decrease when compared with the 1980 report. The proportion of each age group remaining at home is relatively consistent, varying from 59 per cent for 9–11 year olds to 62 per cent for 0–4 year olds.

TABLE 4

Legal status

	No.	%
No legal status	565	60
Section 15 (voluntary care)	25	3
Section 37 (2) Place of Safety	176	19
Section 44(1)(a) Condition of Residence (supervision)	43	4
Section 44(1)(a) Home Supervision (supervision)	74	8
Others	67	7
Total	950	100

Information on legal status refers to the point of registration only. Many of the children who at this point were not the subject of a legal order will have been referred to a children's hearing and will be made the subject of supervision in the future, and obtaining information on such moves is a priority for the department's information system development. Looking at both the information on legal status and accommodation type shows that in the main child abuse work must focus on work with the families rather than separation of the child from the family.

The increase in child abuse referrals has obviously affected the work of the Children's Hearing system, through the increased number of Place of Safety Orders being sought and the need for compulsory measures of care in many cases. The strengths of the Hearing System are, of course, real, and have resulted in the system becoming a focus of interest of several other countries who are seeking to reform their juvenile justice procedures. Notable strengths include the emphasis on the best interest of the child and the degree of discretion accorded Reporters in making decisions on a child or young person's need for compulsory measures of care. The different criterion for evidence means that a balance of probability is acceptable and it is possible to accept abuse has occurred without identifying a perpetrator. Additional strengths include the involvement of the lay public and the provision for family participation. There are, however, intrinsic vulnerabilities within the system, and perhaps these are exposed at their rawest in relation to the management of child abuse cases. Part of the ethos of the Children's Hearing system reflects the belief that the community has a role to play in managing its own problems; it is difficult in practice, however, for lay members of the public, with limited training, to question professional decisions taken elsewhere. The inherent danger is that rather than providing an independent evaluation, the Children's Panel merely ratify decisions taken by professionals on a basis of their ascribed expertise and knowledge. As Kathleen Murray has warned, although the Hearing System is potentially an ideal forum for making decisions about compulsory intervention in cases of child abuse, we have some way to travel before we are in a position to say that the potential is being realised and that the risks of being overwhelmed by bureaucratic procedures are kept to a minimum [22].

Our more recent data do not include detailed information regarding the department's work with the families of children on the register such as information on the time spent on cases and the resources used, but discussions with staff suggest that concern about the lack of time available and the shortfall in resources is still at a high level. Information system developments should enable this information to be collected in future.

Future Developments

Those working on Strathclyde's new procedures, having taken into account both the comments made by staff and the analysis of the department's statistical information, have felt that little change in the procedures was required. The only area clearly requiring substantial review was that of sexual abuse and this has been undertaken.

Child abuse however remains a difficult area and there is a clear need for close monitoring of this area of practice. The region's information system on child abuse at present provides statistical information which although it has illuminated areas requiring policy decisions and allowed district variations to be identified, has been of little or no value operationally. There is a need for accurate information on individual cases to be available to all levels of the department quickly and developments in this area are now under way.

Currently, the main challenge facing Strathclyde and other statutory and voluntary child care agencies in this country is in the field of child sexual abuse [2,23]. Although much has been learned about sexually abusive practices towards children in recent years, it is well to remember that our knowledge base is limited. Difficulties exist in relation to the breadth of definition, as to what actually constitutes a sexual abusive experience, and all attempts at definition must take into account the parameters of time and culture. Few attempts in Great Britain have been made to establish the possible incidence rates of child sexual abuse; although a survey carried out by the Market Opinion and Research International in 1985 [24] projected one in 10, but this definition employed both physical and non-physical contact experiences.

The field of emotional abuse also requires further consideration. Arguments are already well-worn; is it possible to conceptualise emotional abuse as a separate entity? Surely all abusive behaviour towards children incorporates an emotional or psychological abusive element. Is not emotional abuse too elusive a phenomenon to define conceptually and operationally? Most experienced practitioners, however, recognise that emotional abuse exists and will be able to give accounts of families in which constant fault-finding and belittling of a child is an ingrained feature of family interaction. They will be able to give accounts, further, of the consequences for the child, consequences which include hostility, aggression, passive-aggression, dependency and negative self-evaluation [19]. At present, however, it is not a sole criterion for registration in Strathclyde.

The issues of inter-agency communication, staff anxiety and lack of training in dealing with families appear to be no nearer being resolved now than they were ten years ago. Indeed, it has been argued that because of media and public pressure, it has become almost a 'ritual to conclude a case conference with the registration of a child' [25]. The decision of whether or not to seek registration is a difficult one to make. Despite the growing volume of literature on child abuse, little attention has been paid to the impact of the stresses and strains of such work on professionals. It is the professional workers who face families directly and who also work within a complex organisational and professional matrix. It is little wonder that feelings of inadequacy, helplessness, isolation, anger and frustration come to a head. The author of the article referred to above went on to state:

> 'The pressure to cover ourselves from misinformed Press criticism, has led to absurd levels of registrations which, far from alerting us to the need to be particularly vigilant with regard to a particular family has, in fact, deluded us into a false sense of security. In extending the net too far, we run the risk of numbing our senses to the cases to which we should be alerted' [25].

If, however, as our figures suggest, the increase in registrations in Strathclyde is also partly due to greater awareness of sexual abuse and a greater willingness to give credence to children's stories of such abuse, and to a tendency for children to stay longer on the register, then we must be careful that our response to the increasing size of registers is not an over-reaction resulting in our not registering cases where grounds for registration appear to exist.

It is for reasons like these that it is essential to emphasise the need for access to professional supervision which goes beyond routine administering of work for agency needs and affords the opportunity of genuine support based on workers' needs. We require further to acknowledge the importance of access to opportunities for consultancy through the creation of specialist consultancy posts and by making use of individuals outwith the parent agency.

Finally it is important, when considering the training implications of the issues raised in this chapter, that confidential staff counselling services are given some priority, not only for the sake of practitioners themselves, but also for the sake of the families with whom they work.

References

1. Report of the Committee of Inquiry into the Care and Supervision Provided in Relation to Maria Colwell. HMSO, April 1974.

2. Inquiry into Responses to Child Abuse in Cleveland, due to report in 1988.

3. Children's Act, HMSO, 1975.

4. Houghton Committee. Report of the Departmental Committee on the Adoption of Children. Cmnd. 5107, HMSO, 1972.

5. Social Work Scotland Act. HMSO, 1968.

6. Social Work Services Group Circular. SW1/75.

7. Internal departmental reports on the death of a child in care.

8. Strathclyde Regional Council. *Facts About Child Abuse in Strathclyde*. 1980.

9. Gough, D., Boddy, A., Dunning, N. & Stone, F.H. *A Longitudinal Study of Child Abuse in Glasgow. Volume l The Children Who Were Registered*. University of Glasgow, 1987.

10. Skinner, A. & Castle, R. *78 Battered Children*. NSPCC, London, 1969.

11. Elmer, E. & Gregg, G. 'Developmental Characteristics of Abused Children' *Paediatrics*. 40, 1967.

12. Lynch, M. 'Ill Health and the Battered Child' *Lancet*. 1975.

13. Lynch, M. & Roberts, J. 'Predicting Child Abuse and Neglect: Signs of Bonding Failure in the Maternity Hospital' *BMJ*. 1, 1977, 624-626.

14. Kempe, R.S. & Kempe, C.H. *Child Abuse*. Fontana/Open Books, London, 1978.

15. Creighton, S.J. *Child Victims of Physical Abuse*. NSPCC, 1976.

16. Gelles, R.J. *Family Violence*. Sage, Beverley Hills, 1979.

17. Pahl, 1985, quoted in reference 9.

18. Strathclyde Regional Council. *Child Abuse. The Manual of Procedures for Staff of the Social Work Department*. 1985.

19. Deer, B. 'The Unacceptable Face of British Parenthood' *The Sunday Times*. 22nd September 1985.

20. Unpublished report on Scottish Child Abuse Statistics 1985-86, produced for the Association of Directors of Social Work Children and Families Standing Committee.

21. Social Work Services Group Circular SW4/84.

22. Murray, K. 'Children's Hearings and Child Abuse.' Paper presented to a symposium in Glasgow, March 1987.

23. Report on responses to child abuse in Cleveland. *Community Care*. 2.7.87.

24. Market and Opinion Research International, 1985.

25. Corpe, G. 'How Can Registration of Children Protect Them from Abuse?' *Social Work Today*. 31.8.87.

The Changing Role of Foster Parents in Temporary Placements

Isobel Freeman

INTRODUCTION

This chapter looks at the characteristics of children placed with foster families on a temporary basis and considers the extent to which the role of foster parents in temporary placements is and should be developing into a more professional one.

The decrease in the number of children in care at any one point in time in Strathclyde in recent years has not uniformly affected all types of placement, but has resulted largely in a drop in the number of children placed in residential establishments. As a consequence, although in absolute terms the number in foster care has declined very slightly, as a proportion of the total in care it has increased. Of those in care in Strathclyde in 1985 35 per cent were fostered, compared with 38 per cent in Scotland as a whole [1,2]. The proportionate increase is in line with the national trend identified in the early eighties [3,4].

Views on fostering as a form of care have changed greatly over the past decade. Rowe [5], writing about fostering in the eighties, states that:

> 'These days the dictionary definition of fostering as bringing up someone else's child is appropriate for only a proportion of foster home placements.'

When in 1976 the DHSS published their guide to practice in foster care, they reviewed the role of fostering in the past, and reflected on its possible future [6]. The main expansion of the use of fostering to provide short term care, it was suggested, occurred with the coming of the welfare state:

> 'More families who would not have dealt with the old Poor Law authorities, now began to ask for short term reception into care for their children. Public care at the time of illness or confinement became possible and there was an increase in the number of children under five who came into short term care. During the early 1950's it was realised that those young children whose

parents were not able to look after them for short periods, would often receive a more appropriate form of care in a foster home rather than in a residential nursery ... This practice brought the child care services into contact with a different 'set' of foster parents and circumstances for which the service had to adopt new methods of working.'

The subsequent decrease in the use of fostering, in the sixties, is attributed to the awareness that foster placements were breaking down and to an increasing emphasis on prevention, planning and the positive value of good residential care.

The reorganisation of social services departments and the adoption of a generic approach to social work, the report suggested, led to a dispersal of the body of knowledge concerning foster care. However, it anticipated that the mid 1970's would be the beginning of another upsurge:

'Once again there is increased community interest and the establishment of organisations of foster parents has been an important development. Foster care associations are striving to improve the standards of foster care and the status of foster parents. They are asking that they should be seen as equal partners with the staff of social work agencies in their work of caring for children.'

Looking forward from the mid-1970s the report predicted that the next ten years were likely to see many innovative developments in practice. For example, it suggested there would be a development of schemes to place children with exceptional needs and in the training of groups of foster parents to perform particular tasks.

PRACTICE GUIDELINES WITHIN STRATHCLYDE

Within Strathclyde the departmental guidelines have moved away from defining fostering as substitute parenting, defining it instead as 'Situations in which a child is cared for in a family setting in the community' [7].

They go on to state:

'Fostering in itself is not a single identifiable method of care, its many forms are designed to meet the individual needs of children and have in common only the fact that they provide care in a family setting.'

Fostering placements are divided into two main types, permanent and temporary placements, but within each of these two groups, placements differ with families utilising different skills and qualities to meet the different needs of children in care.

Placements are defined as temporary when there is a definite plan, either to return the child to his family, or to move him to an alternative placement. The guidelines describe four types of temporary placements:

(1) Emergency placements
(2) Pre-adoption placements
(3) Respite/holiday placements
(4) Task-centred placements.

Within the latter category, general tasks are identified:

(i) Providing a bridge between a disruption or residential care and a permanent family placement.
(ii) Assessment in the community.
(iii) Providing an alternative to residential care for teenagers including offenders.
(iv) Providing care for severely emotionally or behaviourally disturbed children who cannot be directly adopted.

In Strathclyde, therefore, foster care is not defined in a time-limited way, but in terms of whether a move home or to an alternative placement is planned. A number of writers [8] recognise the following classification of fostering:

(i) short term (up to 8 weeks)
(ii) intermediate (3 months to 2 years) including treatment fostering
(iii) long term.

The first two categories are temporary forms of care and both would be included in Strathclyde's classification of temporary placements.

RESEARCH INTO TEMPORARY PLACEMENTS

As Tunstill [4] pointed out, although there has been much research and discussion of permanent fostering and fostering in general, few studies have looked specifically at short-term placements, although this situation is now changing. Tibbenham's [9] investigation in South Devon (1980–81) included 49 short term placements. More recent projects carried out by Berridge and Cleaver [10] and Rowe [11] cover placements of varying types. When comparing the results of such studies it is important to be clear about which types of placements are covered. Berridge and Cleaver, for example, looked at short-term and intermediate placements separately, but both sections would require to be referred to when comparing their study with our analysis. This chapter presents data from the department's information system and from a more detailed study of a sample of 99 temporary foster placements carried out as part of a wider examination of disruption in all placements [12].

Tunstill [4] comments that research into fostering in Britain and the United States has traditionally been concerned with the question of breakdown. Although the Strathclyde study focussed on disruption, it nevertheless raised wider practice issues and pointed to ways in which social workers and foster parents could work together more effectively. It is on these issues rather than disruption which this chapter focusses.

Characteristics of Children in Temporary Foster Care

At present (1987) there are around 600 children in temporary foster care. Fifty per cent are aged under five, 23 per cent between five and eight, 11 per cent between nine and 11 and 15 per cent over 12. Many of the children have been in care for some time; over 40 per cent were received into care in 1985 or before. The proportion who had been in their existing placement since 1985 or before was slightly lower (32 per cent).

In 1986, 859 children were received into care and placed directly into non-related temporary foster placements. Just over half were received into care together with one or more siblings; therefore the children represented fewer than 600 families. The majority of the placements involved young children, with 65 per cent under five and 29 per cent aged 5–11. Only 6 per cent were aged 12 or more. The proportion of those in the older age group fostered at any one point in time is greater than the proportion of those received into care who are fostered, since younger children tend to spend shorter periods in care.

Despite their youth, over a third of the children had been in care before. Almost half came from families with no male carer present, and the natural father was present in the home in only 27 per cent of cases.

The insecurity of many of the children placed in temporary foster care was demonstrated by the more detailed investigation of the 99 placements referred to above [12]. All temporary placements lasting more than four weeks made in a four month period were examined. The study involved interviews with social workers, foster parents, natural parents and the children themselves, and produced a very detailed picture of this sample of placements which complements the information on the much larger number of placements available from the information system.

At the beginning of their placement not only had several of the children been in care before, but it was also found that around half had experienced moves between carers when not in care. Thus there was a lack of continuity of care for many children. Only 17 of the children's mothers were living with their husbands (not necessarily the child's natural father), and 23 with their cohabitee. The majority of mothers were living on their own. In only four cases was the relationship between both natural parents said to be good at the time the placement was made. Siblings also moved in and out of the family home. Of the 76 mothers who had children, only 25 had some of the children living with them. It is clear therefore that it is not only coming in and out of local authority care which has caused disruption in the family lives of the children studied. They have also experienced changes in their own family situation through the separation of parents, the introduction of a cohabitee or a stepfather, and the movement of siblings in and out of the home. The study of parental and family contact with children in care, carried out by the Dartington research unit, also found a high level of family mobility [13].

Reasons for Coming into Care

The vast majority of the 859 children placed directly into temporary foster care in 1986 were admitted on an emergency basis. Almost a fifth were received into care by the department's out-of-hours service, and almost two-thirds were described by the social worker as unplanned admissions. The most common reasons for admission were illness (physical illness (13 per cent), mental illness (9 per cent) or pregnancy (3 per cent)), or deteriorating relationships between child and carer(s) (7 per cent), abuse and neglect (9 per cent), lack of parental care (14 per cent), desertion (6 per cent) and drunkenness (9 per cent)). Six per cent were pre-adoption placements. The majority of placements were made on a voluntary basis. Thirty two per cent were subject to a place of safety order.

Most of the temporary foster placements can be classified into two main groups:
1. those providing respite care, generally on a voluntary basis
2. those providing emergency care in situations where the child requires a place of safety.

The more detailed analysis of the 99 placements which looked at admissions to placement rather than care produced a similar picture although there was also a small number of placements resulting from transfers and either

a) involving an attempt to provide the experience of family life for older children who had been in care for some time; or
b) involving a move to a placement which it was felt was more suitable for carrying out work towards rehabilitation.

From an analysis of reasons for reception into care it appears therefore that within Strathclyde temporary fostering placements in the main are providing respite and emergency care for younger children. Such care, although generally seen as less demanding than providing care for severely handicapped children or older children defined as requiring residential supervision, often requires foster parents to perform fairly complex tasks calling for a high degree of skill. This high level of skill is not always recognised.

Placements Providing Respite

Among the group of placements providing respite, the reasons given for the initial reception into care was most commonly 'deteriorating relationship between child and carer' and the physical or mental illness of the carer. The need for care or protection was referred to in a small number of cases only. In the majority of respite cases the foster parents were not asked to undertake any specific work with the children; in about a quarter treatment was referred to and in a similar number of cases assessment was stated as a purpose of the placement. In the cases where treatment and assessment were mentioned as placement purposes, often little more detail about the tasks the foster parents were expected to perform were given. Some examples of the social workers' description of the purpose of placement are given below:

> *Graham aged 12:* 'The reception into care was planned because his Gran was going into hospital. It was to provide substitute family care on a temporary basis. It was also to give him a better experience than he had at home.'

> *John aged 1:* 'His father had left his mother who felt she couldn't cope and pleaded with us to receive the child into care. The purpose of the placement was to provide a stable environment for the child.'

> *Matthew aged 5:* 'He was received into care at his mother's request. She felt she might assault him. The purpose was short term relief for the mother who was mentally ill.'

Placements Providing Refuge

In all these placements the need for care or protection was mentioned. In almost a third of the cases deteriorating relationships with carers were referred to, and in a quarter, drunkenness. Again foster parents were not usually asked to undertake any specific work although treatment was a factor in about a quarter of these cases and assessment in one-sixth. The following descriptions, provided by social workers, give an illustration of the circumstances in which these children came into care.

> *Neil aged less than 1:* 'The father dropped the baby while drunk and the baby was taken to the hospital by his mother with a fractured skull. The purpose

of the placement was to satisfy legal requirements and to allow us time to discuss the father's alcohol problem and to set up counselling. I was angry that the legal proceedings took so long, but I needed the child out of the way while I worked with the father.'

Aileen aged 2: 'She was received into care to allow us to investigate allegations of abuse.'

Brian aged 5: 'Brian and his brother were received into care because they were left unattended. The placement was to let the natural parents sort themselves out and provide the boys with stability.'

Admissions under place of safety orders ranged from those where abuse of some sort had been identified, to placements where allegations of lack of care had been made and investigation was required. Looking at the details of the admissions, it was clear that to many social workers, the time which investigations and the legal processes took was a matter of concern, and it did appear that children could be in care for several weeks while investigations took place into what could eventually turn out to be unfounded allegations. This reinforces the findings of McCluskey and Fegan's analysis [14].

Tasks in Respite and Emergency Care

Although the children were young, many had experienced frequent lapses in the continuity of their care. Recent research by Vernon and Fruin [15] in England and Wales and Denham [16] in Scotland described three groups of cases as child behaviour, service to the family and rescue from the family placements. The cases in the sample involved examples of 'rescue from the family' and 'service to the family' cases although classification into these two groups is by no means clear cut and most cases involve elements of both. As was seen above, only a minority of placements were clearly defined as task-centred. Defining the placements as emergency and respite, or service to the family, or rescue from the family placements focusses on the beginning of the placement, yet in temporary placements work towards their end must begin immediately. In the majority of these placements work towards rehabilitation is carried out by the social worker but the foster parents have a lot to offer in this direction. In placements where plans for rehabilitation fail, preparation for a permanent placement requires to be undertaken. Again foster parents can provide much of this preparation.

Use of Contracts

Contracts have been seen as useful social work tools for a number of years [17] yet only a small number of the 99 placements examined in detail had involved drawing up a contract, although the introduction of new guidelines should have led to an improvement in this situation. Of particular concern is the tendency for social workers and foster parents to underestimate the length of the placement required, and this in some occasions can result in a change of placement which would not have been required had a realistic estimate been made. The value of contracts in permanent placements is stressed by Aldgate and Hawley [18]. In temporary placements it appears that the need for clearly defined contracts is as great, if not greater than, in permanent placements. Such contracts should include information on expected duration in care but make clear the department's expectations of the foster parents in situations where things do not go according to plan.

Social Work Support

Support is clearly also as important in temporary as in permanent placements. A study carried out by the DHSS in 1981 [19] felt this area of work could be improved and suggested that authorities with a link worker system, i.e. where foster parents are provided with their own social work support rather than being expected to rely on the social workers responsible for the children placed with them, were providing better support. Within Strathclyde a link worker system is operating in most parts of the region. The foster parents, however, generally had some criticisms about lack of support, particularly from the child's social worker, citing infrequent visiting, failure to return phone calls and failure to do as promised in the time scale arranged. Some social workers, as would be expected, were found more supportive than others.

> 'I like fostering, it gives us different experiences. The only problem is if you get a rotten social worker. Sometimes I ask to see the social worker before I see the child just to have an idea what I am letting myself in for' (Foster Parent).

Colleagues or Clients?

Within Strathclyde many foster parents were aware of a changing role and the changing expectations the department had of them. At the time the interviews were undertaken, however, there appeared to be some confusion among staff over whether foster parents were colleagues or clients, with different social workers treating them in different ways. The comments made by social workers themselves illustrate this:

> 'The foster parents wanted to know a lot more than they needed to' (Social Worker).

> 'I tried to give them a clearer understanding of the Department's legal rights and the needs of the child. We had the foster parents closely involved in decision making' (Social Worker).

Involvement in this case meant keeping them informed but some foster parents themselves were beginning to want to play an even greater part in making decisions.

> 'If the foster parents are having a lot of natural parent visits they should have a bit more say about when this child is ready to go back and when the natural mother is ready to have him' (Foster Parent).

In some cases such changes appear to be already happening.

> 'Things are changing in fostering, we're more involved in reviews etc. now and things are beginning to get discussed with us' (Foster Parent).

Given that they are generally involved with several social workers, more consistency in the treatment of temporary foster parents is necessary. It is accepted that their abilities vary, but if critical assessments of foster parents were undertaken regularly and made available to all social workers considering placing a child with them, a more standardised approach could be adopted. At the time of the study, assessments provided limited information about foster parents' abilities and were often out of date. The adoption of new procedures involving regular reviews of foster parents should help overcome this problem.

Access

Increasing emphasis on the need for parental access has greatly affected the foster parents' role. Our investigation of temporary placements, like the Dartington research [13] on access, demonstrated the difficulties faced when trying to maintain contact between children in care and their parents. For the majority of the children in the sample it was their attachment to their natural mother which was important, as most had already lost contact with their natural father. Although social workers felt that the relationship between natural mother and child left room for improvement, in most cases there clearly was an attachment which needed to be maintained.

Maintaining this contact when the child has been placed in the foster family clearly posed problems. Holman [20] in 1980 discussed exclusive and inclusive concepts of fostering. Professionals' views on the extent to which fostering should be inclusive, i.e. maintain the child's sense of the past and where possible develop the relationship with the natural family, still vary although more workers are recognising the value of links with the past. Even where it is advocated that society must take over the parental role [21] this generally should not result in the terminating of parental ties. In temporary fostering situations where in the majority of cases rehabilitation is planned, access must always be maintained. Social workers are well aware of the difficulties which can arise [22,23,24].

At the time this research was being carried out, new policies on access were being introduced. Many foster parents recruited at a time when no pressure was put on them to become involved with natural parents found these changes difficult to cope with. Some disliked being involved with natural parents, rejecting any access arrangements involving them. Where access arrangements were made, problems often arose because they were not clear. Natural parents in particular often thought the agreement reached had been more flexible than it actually was. Often arrangements for access were not made at the beginning of the placement but a few days into the placement, and it was only then that difficulties came to light, e.g. the foster parents' reluctance to have natural parents visit, no suitable buses, etc. When this happened the social worker was left with the dilemma of either moving the child, thus disrupting the continuity of care, or accepting a placement with less than suitable access arrangements.

Transport problems appeared to be common, but sometimes the transport problems referred to masked deeper problems. Foster families see children who have been badly treated by their parents and occasional bad experiences may make them wary of all natural parents. As one social worker put it, when trying to understand a foster family's reluctance to allow natural parent contact:

> 'The foster parents possibly didn't realise that the individual cases are quite different. This may be the department's fault. The foster parents had experienced children who had been seriously injured or abused and no-one explained to them that not all cases were the same' (Social Worker).

Previous studies have looked at the relationship between social class and disruptions. George [25] found no significant relationship, while Parker [26] found that the lower the social class of the foster parents, the more likely the placement is to be successful.

Our study, although showing no statistical relationship, found problems resulting from differences in the living standards of the foster families and natural families.

'We didn't like the placement, they were spoiling him. They were richer than us' (Natural Parent).

Role difficulties were also a problem during visits, e.g. who should discipline the child if he or she did something wrong, the natural mother whose child it was, or the foster mother who was caring for the child at the time and in whose house the visits often took place? This problem is referred to in discussions of access in permanent placements [23], and in such cases the natural parents have to be helped relinquish the day-to-day parental role, but the situation is much less clear cut when rehabilitation is planned. Problems arose especially if the foster parents and the natural parents differed in their views about what was and what was not acceptable behaviour and how unacceptable behaviour should be dealt with.

Since the fieldwork for the research into temporary placements was undertaken it is possible that improvements in arranging access may have occurred, but more recent information suggests this is not the case. Analysis of the receptions into temporary foster care in 1986 does not leave much room for optimism. In 16 per cent of cases daily contact was agreed, and in 22 per cent, weekly contact. In 19 per cent some other agreement was reached, such as contact as required. In almost a quarter of the cases no arrangement for contact was made at the time of reception into care, and in a further quarter it was stated that no contact with parents would take place. Information on reviews showed that where reviews were held in the foster parents' home the natural family were much less likely to attend, suggesting problems surrounding the natural parent and foster parent relationship are still significant.

The Placement Endings

The importance of placement endings and the skills needed to ensure they are successful was referred to earlier. Previous studies have generally defined 'success' in fostering in terms of whether or not a disruption has occurred, but in temporary placements which are planned to end in any case such a definition is often difficult to apply. Similar problems were referred to by Tibbenham [9]. The study of the 99 placements looked at all endings of temporary placements rather than simply focussing on breakdown, thus enabling some discussion of 'success' to take place. Approximately a third of the placements ended as a result of a voluntary agreement that the child return home. In the vast majority of these cases the social workers, foster parents and natural parents agreed that the purpose of the placement had been met. In a few cases the natural parents appeared to be reluctant to resume the parental role but were persuaded by social workers to do so, and in a few cases the social worker was reluctant to end the placement, but not to such an extent that they felt compulsory measures of care were warranted.

A further third of the placements ended as the result of a Children's Hearing decision to return the child home. On only one occasion was such a decision not in line with the social worker's plan for the child. All but one of these placements could be described therefore as having ended with the successful rehabilitation of the child to the care of its natural family (although the quality of this care will clearly vary). Interviews with natural parents after the return of their child did suggest that in some cases, especially where reception into care had been voluntary, social work support was withdrawn too quickly in the view of the natural parents. The need to provide continued support to natural families after rehabilitation should therefore be emphasised.

The remainder of the placements ended in the transfer of the child to a new placement. Transfers were required for a number of reasons:

1) because a permanent family was found for the child
2) because a more appropriate placement was found enabling
   a) better parental access arrangements
   b) siblings to be placed together
3) because the researched placement broke down.

It was often difficult to be sure whether transfers described as a move to a more appropriate placement were motivated by the advantages of the new placement or problems in the old one. A particular problem appeared to be the length of time placements where rehabilitation had failed could last.

Dougie aged 12

> *Foster parents' interview:* 'The placement was planned to last for six months and did. We felt angry and sad when he left. It was because of departmental inefficiency. We had a good relationship with him. The department took too long to process the application of his long term foster parents.'

> *Social worker's interview:* It ended after six months but not as planned. The foster parents were adamant that they wouldn't offer longer periods. I felt that this was unfortunate because the children were doing well and beginning to establish a relationship.'

Alistair aged less than 1

Foster parents' interview: He left because he'd been here too long and we were all getting too attached and it wasn't fair on Alistair. He was to spend a fortnight with his mother in July while we were on holiday as preparation for him going home. This fell through and the plan changed from rehabilitation to long-term care. We decided to ask that he move after the holidays.'

Social worker's interview: The placement ended because the foster parents realised it was likely that the child would remain in care and they were growing very attached to him and he to them. I felt it was in his best interest to end the placement. The ending was not as originally planned, it had been planned to take him back to his mother. New foster parents were being selected and the child was introduced to them. From the child's point of view it was a satisfactory transfer, he got to know the new foster parents and was happy to move. I wouldn't call it a disruption.'

Berridge and Cleaver [10], in their intensive study of 10 breakdowns, suggested endings are often negotiated. Our findings to a large extent reflect this view.

Tunstill [4] in her review of research suggested that more recent investigations of breakdown have found behaviour problems of the child to be of key importance. Studies carried out in Cleveland, Essex, Strathclyde and South Devon all referred to behaviour [27,28,29,9]. Our more recent study, although finding behaviour to be important, found foster parents varied greatly in terms of the range of behaviour with which they could cope.

Behaviour problems existed in almost all placements to a greater or lesser extent but many placements where severe problems existed continued as planned, while several of the placements which broke down involved little or no problematic behaviour from the children. In fact, reading the detailed case studies, it appears that inadequate preparation of foster parents for the role they were being asked to play, or the failure of the department to plan or implement plans, were often more influential in causing placements to break down than the child's behaviour.

Calculating a breakdown rate is difficult but it does appear that although around one in three placements involved transferring the child to a new placement, only around one in five placements break down, i.e. do not end in accordance with the social work plan. The remainder of the transfers were the result of developments in the care plan for the child. As Rowe [5,30] points out when comparing breakdown rates, it is important that the types of placement compared are similar. More important than calculating a breakdown rate is identifying the difficulties which can be experienced by those involved in all placements whether they end 'successfully' and 'according to plan' or not. The need to warn foster parents of these potential problems and provide them with the training required to deal with them must be recognised. Having said this, it must be acknowledged that although we can always do better, the majority of temporary foster placements are providing good quality care for as long as it is needed.

CONCLUSION

Strathclyde's definition of temporary fostering includes those requiring short term emergency or respite care and those requiring what has been described in some of the literature as treatment fostering. The majority of children placed in temporary foster care are in the younger age group and require respite and/or emergency care. The previous care experience and changing family circumstances of many of even the very young children, and the need to work towards rehabilitation, or where this fails, preparation for a permanent family, can require from the foster parents a high level of skill.

The introduction to this chapter referred to the DHSS guide to foster care [6] produced in 1976 and its comments on the increasing professionalisation of the foster parents' role. Further moves in this direction, particularly greater consistency in the expectations social workers have of foster parents, are still required.

For foster parents recruited some time ago the changing expectations of their role may be difficult to cope with and reassessment and retraining may be required. In the case of newly recruited foster parents, our expectations must be clear from the beginning. The recently-produced boarding out regulations [31] stress the need for clearly defined contracts to be made with foster parents, not just regarding individual placements, but their role in general. The implementation of these guidelines should help accelerate the developments in the role of temporary foster parents.

References

1. Social Work Services Group. 'Children in Care 1985' *Statistical Bulletin.* March, 1987.

2 Strathclyde Regional Council. 'Needs and Resources.' 1985.

3 Knapp, M. 'The Resource Consequences of Changes in Child Care Policy: Foster Care and Intermediate Treatment'. In Lishman, J. (Ed.) *Working with Children. Research Highlights*, No. 6, Aberdeen University, 1983, reprint edition Jessica Kingsley, 1987.

4 Tunstill, J. 'Fostering: Direct Work During Placement'. In Lishman, J. (Ed.) *Working with Children. Research Highlights*, No. 6, Aberdeen University, 1983, reprint edition Jessica Kingsley, 1987.

5 Rowe, J. *Fostering in the Eighties*. British Agencies for Adoption and Fostering, London, 1983.

6 Department of Health and Social Security. *Foster Care*. 1976.

7 Strathclyde Regional Council. 'Fostering Guidelines.' 1985.

8 Triseliotis, J. Unpublished paper on the nature of foster care, 1987.

9 Exeter Social Services Department. 'A Study of Terminations of Placements in 1980–81.' 1981.

10. Berridge, D. & Cleaver, H. 'Summary of Findings of a Study of Fostering Breakdowns.' (To be published October 1987 by Blackwell).

11. Rowe, J. *A Study of Placement Outcomes*. British Agencies for Adoption and Fostering (forthcoming).

12. This study was made possible through a grant made by Social Work Services Group to F.E. Edwards. The fieldwork was supervised by Dr. James Russell, Senior Research Officer to the project, and the analysis of data and writing up of the project was undertaken by James Russell, Helen Brownlie and Isobel Freeman. A full report on the study of temporary placements will be published by Social Work Services Group, November 1987.

13. Millham, S., Bullock, R., Hosie, K. and Haak, M. *Lost in Care*. Gower, Aldershot, 1986.

14. See McCluskey, F. and Fegan, M. in this volume.

15. Vernon, J. & Fruin, D. *In Care*. National Children's Bureau, 1986.

16. Denham, E.J. *Social Work Decision Making in Child Care*. National Children's Bureau, SWSG, May 1985.

17. Sheldon, B. *The Use of Contracts in Social Work*. British Association of Social Workers, London, 1980.

18. Aldgate, J. & Hawley, D. 'Preventing Disruption in Long Term Foster Care' *Adoption and Fostering*. 10, 3, 1986.

19. Department of Health and Social Security. 'A Study of the Boarding Out of Children' *Social Work Service*, 1981.

20. Holman, R. 'Exclusive and Inclusive Concepts of Fostering'. In Triseliotis, J. (Ed.) *New Developments in Foster Care and Adoption*. Routledge and Kegan Paul, London, 1980.

21. Fox, L. 'Two Value Positions in Recent Child Care Law and Practice' *British Journal of Social Work*. 12, 1982.

22. Gilmour, I. 'Parental Access in Scotland' *Adoption and Fostering*. 10, 3, 1986.

23. Johnson, D. 'Access: the Natural Parents' Dilemma' *Adoption and Fostering*. 10, 3, 1986.

24. Gibson, P. & Parsloe, P. 'What Stops Parental Access?' *Adoption and Fostering*. 8, 1, 1984.

25. George, V. *Foster Care*. Routledge & Kegan Paul, London, 1976.

26. Parker, R. *Decisions in Child Care*. Allen & Unwin, London, 1966.

27. Cleveland Social Services Department. 'Survey of Foster Placements.' 1981.

28. Essex Social Services Department. 'Foster Home Breakdown Survey.' 1982.

29. Strathclyde Regional Council. 'Fostering and Adoption Disruption in Strathclyde.' 1982.

30. Rowe, J. 'Fostering Outcomes: Interpreting Breakdown Rates' *Adoption and Fostering*. 11, 1, 1987.

31. The Boarding-Out and Fostering of Children (Scotland) Regulations 1985.

Issues in Baby Adoption

Stuart Montgomery and Gordon Findlay

INTRODUCTION

This chapter sets out to discuss a number of issues surrounding the adoption of babies and young infants, in particular focussing on the selection of adoptive parents, and it reports some of the findings of a recent empirical investigation. It is suggested that although the major emphasis of contemporary adoption work has been upon older children and those with 'special needs', baby adoption continues to raise important questions of policy and practice.

In Scotland, as in the rest of Britain, adoption practice has undergone considerable change during the last twenty years. Once almost exclusively concerned with placing healthy, uncomplicated babies with childless couples, adoption is now the preferred option for a much wider range of children. A full explanation of this change would have to take account of several strategic shifts in child care policy, such as the development of a child-centred approach and the growing preference for family-based over institutional provision for all children in care, including those with special needs [1,2]. It would also have to encompass broader social changes affecting the adoption 'market'.

For despite a continuing increase in the number of illegitimate births, the supply of babies available for adoption has fallen quite dramatically. In England and Wales in 1984, for example, there were just over 2,200 adoptions of children aged under two years, compared with about 6,500 in 1974 [3]. Within Scotland the most recent published statistics relating to this age-group show a decrease from 422 adoption orders in 1979 to 352 in 1983 [4], and figures for Strathclyde Region point to an even steeper drop with 68 children aged under two being placed in 1985, in contrast to 149 in 1981 [5]. Jane Rowe reviews factors responsible for this overall reduction in her book *Yours by Choice* [6]. She describes how, in the post-war period, rather harsh social attitudes together with severe practical and material obstacles to single parenthood led many unmarried mothers to conclude that the only course open to them was to place their child for adoption. However:

> 'By the early 1970s the pattern was changing. Social attitudes to illegitimacy became kinder, housing shortages eased a little, and welfare payments improved. Whereas the pressure on single mothers had previously been in favour of placing their babies for adoption, now the pressure was on them to keep the child. "You wouldn't be so awful as to give your baby away would you?" became the prevailing attitude.'

At the same time more reliable methods of contraception and the possibility of abortion were reducing the number of unwanted babies born to mothers who were unable to keep them.

But, as Rowe acknowledges, although the supply of babies has dwindled, the demand for them has continued unabated, and all agencies have been faced with the need to respond to that demand in ways that ensure good standards of child care while remaining sensitive to the needs and feelings of prospective adopters. It was against this background that, in July 1986 Strathclyde Regional Council's adoption sub-committee decided to recommend an age limit for couples applying to adopt babies or very young children.

Although presented in the main as a straightforwardly administrative piece of demand management, the proposal attracted considerable (though by no means unanimous) support on practice grounds. Arguments for placing young children only with young couples included the following: the biological mothers usually want this; younger couples have more energy to cope, and to engage in play, with young children; the children will grow up with parents no older than those of their peers, and will not therefore feel 'different'. There is some research evidence to support this argument, with both McWhinnie [7] and Kornitzer [8] reporting more successful outcomes when the adoptive mothers were under 40. Similarly, in a study of adoption outcome among 'hard to place' children, Triseliotis and Russell found that placement with older couples (in this instance, over the age of 45) 'tends to decrease the amount of satisfaction felt with the adoption experience' [9]. These authors are talking about the *children's* satisfaction with the adoption experience, but Rowe suggests that older couples may themselves become dissatisfied, at least in the long run [6]:

> 'Most women of 45 are quite capable of looking after an infant even if they do find the broken nights and constant washing rather tiring. Not so many of them at 55 or 60 have the energy and patience to cope with the tiresome ways of a teenage son or daughter.'

Whatever its rationale, the move was unexceptional; all other Scottish local authorities operated limits which broadly matched Strathclyde's proposal to consider only couples whose younger partner was under 35 [10]. Perhaps more unusual was that this ruling was to be retrospective, affecting not only couples considering a first application, but also those already approved. (The basis for this lay once again in the acute shortage of available babies: it was estimated that it would take several years to place babies with all the approved couples, by which time many would be well into their forties). There were 31 couples in that situation, some of whom had been formally approved several years previously but were still awaiting a placement. Their understandable dismay and anger led to a fierce protest that caught considerable media attention, and ensured a cautious approach when the proposal was brought before the full Social Work Committee for ratification.

Their response was to set aside the recommendation temporarily to allow time for further deliberation, and more information was requested about the characteristics of all couples who had applied to adopt since the formation of Strathclyde Region. Because the administrative records of the adoption sections were still almost entirely manual, it was necessary to mount an ad hoc survey. Constraints on time meant that the survey was more hurried than we would have liked, and it focussed mainly on the rather narrow issue of the ages of prospective adopters, but its findings nevertheless had implications for adoption policy that were more wide-ranging than we expected [11]. After a brief description of the survey and its impact on the age issue, this chapter discusses some of these implications.

THE SURVEY

Conducted during August 1986 the survey looked at people who, since May 1975, had applied to adopt one or more children. Couples not proceeding beyond an initial enquiry were excluded, as were applicants still waiting to be assessed and those seeking to adopt a child already in their foster care. The inquiry was therefore limited to people making definite application to adopt an unknown child. Given a rather short deadline for the report to Committee, it was impossible to include every couple meeting these criteria, so a 25 per cent sample was drawn from each Division. Information from registers and files was extracted by Divisional staff, and recorded on a standard questionnaire; the data were analysed using the Council's mainframe computer.

A total of 605 couples were included, with Glasgow Division having the highest number at 183, and Argyll/Dunbarton the lowest at 75. (Remember that these figures represent only a one-in-four sample). It was found that 552 had been approved, of whom 445 had already had a child placed. In 333 instances a child under two years had been placed; the ages of their adoptive parents are shown in the table below.

TABLE 1

Age at placement of adopters of children aged under two

	Mothers		Fathers	
	No.	%	No.	%
Under 25	2	0.6	1	0.3
25–29	76	22.8	44	13.2
30–34	151	45.3	136	40.8
35–39	79	23.7	107	32.1
40 or over	14	4.2	35	10.5
No information	11	3.3	10	3.0
Total	333	100.0	333	100.0

It can be seen that almost 28 per cent of the adoptive mothers and over 40 per cent of the adoptive fathers of very young children had been older than the new cut-off limit when their child was placed. Clearly, then, the proposed age restriction suggested a significant shift in practice. Taking account of this, and of other considerations, Committee overturned the earlier decision, and ruled that an age limit of 40 years, for the younger partner, would now be imposed (but that it would not apply retrospectively). The sub-committee's other main recommendation – that baby adoption be centralised as a Regional, rather than Divisional, function – was, however, accepted.

DIVISIONAL VARIATION

Of as much interest as the main findings themselves, particularly in view of the proposals for centralisation, was the survey's evidence of variations in practice across the Region, relating not only to the central issue of the age of adopters but also to the broader gatekeeping functions of Divisional Adoption Case Committees. Although the Case Committee (or 'Panel') structure – with a group of health, psychological and social work staff, chaired by an elected member or by the Divisional fieldwork manager – was the same in each Division, they appeared to operate in different ways. The first aspect of this concerned the initial selection of prospective adopters.

Selection of Applicants

Taking the Region as a whole, fully 91 per cent of all applications were approved by the Panels, but Divisional figures ranged from 78 per cent to 99 per cent, as can be seen in the following table, where the five Divisions are labelled 'A' to 'E'.

TABLE 2

Case Committees' decisions (percentages)

	Division					
	A	B	C	D	E	TOTAL
Approved	91	99	97	78	88	91
Rejected	7	1	3	14	10	6
Withdrew before decision made	1	–	–	8	–	2
Pending	1	–	–	–	–	0.5
Other	–	–	–	–	2	0.5
Total	100	100	100	100	100	100

Two major questions, or rather clusters of questions, are prompted by such differences, concerning first the organisational aspects of selection and, second, the basis of selection itself.

Organisational Aspects

Local variations in selection policy had been identified as long ago as 1978, when the report of a member – officer group review of child care practice commented:

> 'All Divisions seemed to have their own policy of recruitment of adopters, each incorporating different methods of initial selection for vetting and it would seem appropriate that the Region consider some overall policy in this matter' [12].

It would have been surprising, indeed, if standard practices had existed at that time, given that Strathclyde Region had been created as an administrative unit only three years earlier, out of a number of previously separate local authorities. Certainly, considerable differences had been found in other parts of the UK. For example, in a survey carried out in the early 1960s, Goodacre reported that the 14 statutory and voluntary agencies active in her study area (in England) operated a wide range of organisational arrangements [13]. She found that although all agencies complied with the legal requirement to place final responsibility for the selection of applicants in the hands of their case committees, the latter differed greatly in composition and outlook. Membership in some was almost entirely limited to social work professionals, but was mostly lay people in others. Perhaps as a result, there were divergent views on how to divide responsibilities between case committee members and the social workers carrying out assessments. Though not absent from the local authority departments, these differences were most evident among the voluntary societies:

> 'Some society committees were described as "working", and by this was meant that they took an active part in vetting applicants, either by visiting their homes or seeing them before the committee. Other committees limited their function to the endorsement of their fieldworkers' recommendations. As one secretary said: "I can be sure that in ninety-nine cases out of a hundred, my committee agrees to my proposals." In her case, verbal reports only were presented. Other committees decided nothing before making a detailed study of full written as well as verbal reports.'

The influence of Strathclyde's member-officer group's recommendation that recruitment procedures be standardised is discernible in the 'Adoption Policy and Practice Guidelines' issued by the Council in July 1980 [14]. These stipulated that Divisions would no longer have authority to close waiting lists periodically, and that they would henceforward operate the same recording system. The main emphasis of the paragraphs concerning selection, however, was upon the primacy of the Case Committee as the decision-making body in each Division, and important limitations on the discretion of social workers were laid down. It was stressed that:

> '... no individual social worker has the authority to advise enquirers that their application cannot be taken up.'

A later section elaborated the proper procedure:

> 'If it is competent for an application to be taken up, Form A2 should be issued for completion by applicants. When a completed form has been received, this is regarded as the stage of FORMAL APPLICATION and reports on ALL formal applications must be submitted in due course to the Adoption Case Committee. Therefore, if applicants subsequently withdraw a report outlining the reasons must be submitted to the Case Committee.' (stress original)

While not denying the social worker's expertise the Guidelines appeared to be saying that the worker's role is confined to assessing applications, and does not extend to negotiating with couples about whether a formal application should in fact be lodged. An observer using this model as a framework for interpreting the Divisional variation seen in Table 2 might therefore be critical of the 99 per cent rate, holding that it shows too lenient an attitude, and that with rejection so rare it would be more cost-effective to dispense with the Case Committee (and perhaps also, by implication, the social workers) and simply approve all applicants who met the eligibility criteria and passed the police check. From this perspective the 78 per cent rate reflects a more responsible attitude to selection.

A contrasting model can however be seen in Joan Cooper's report of her survey of 'current issues in fostering and adoption', undertaken in 1977 [15]. She describes the development of a 'casework approach to selection' of foster and adoptive parents:

> 'The process involves the family and, later, relatives or significant friends and helpers in a two way selection process which allows the family and agency to withdraw without acute feelings of resentment and rejection. With this framework initial discussions provide opportunities for exchange of information between the family and the agency and for exploration on a 'no obligation' basis. Once the exploratory stage is completed, the formal application is introduced and signifies some commitment on either side to justify the pursuit of the health and character inquiries.'

Within Cooper's model, therefore, the 78 per cent figure in Table 2 indicates an unnecessarily high rate of rejection, and calls into question the role of the social workers and the Advisers vis a vis the rejected applicants, wondering why they did not 'counsel out' more couples at an early stage in order to spare them the distress and uncertainty of assessment, as well as the eventual hurt of rejection. In this light, a high acceptance rate might be evidence of sensitive social work practice, rather than of a slack Case Committee.

We do not mean to suggest that these contrasting models were applied in an exclusive and unchanging fashion in different Divisions. Over the period covered by the survey the 'casework' approach was growing in popularity throughout the Region; this is evident from the department's *fostering* guidelines, issued in 1985, which observe [16]:

> 'In recent years, the concept of "vetting" applicants has been superseded by the more helpful process of assessment and preparation of applicants ... The process will contain elements of information sharing, evaluation and assessment, and preparation for placement ...'

What seems clear, though, is that this trend did not equally affect all parts of the Region, and that, Guidelines not withstanding, different approaches tended to be taken in different areas. Since these variations were not explicitly formulated or monitored, it is unlikely that they have ensured the highest standards of practice. Furthermore, the likelihood that applicants will have received different treatment because of their area of residence is a matter of concern.

The decision to centralise the administration and processing of baby adoptions, referred to above, will greatly reduce the risk of such inequities in the future, but it cannot be assumed that this change will of itself entirely clarify the relationship between Case Committees and social workers. Difficulties with that relationship have been such a perennial topic (e.g. Goodacre [13], Triseliotis [17], Jacka [18]) that we must assume that they will persist. Our own hope is that continuing monitoring of recruitment practice, through routine information systems, will enable problems to be identified at an early stage.

Finally, and regrettably, it has to be said that the survey was better at provoking such questions than answering them. Partly this was inevitable: a full insight on how applicants are processed and filtered would demand a much more detailed investigation, and one with a strong qualitative component. Even so, the inclusion of a questionnaire item about the social worker's recommendation as well as the Panel's decision, would have permitted some interesting analysis. So, too, would better quality data on the initial enquiries about adoption; analysis of the proportions of enquiries developing into formal applications might have been revealing, but the recording systems could not furnish comprehensive details. (The questionnaire did ask for enquiry dates for the definite applications, but few were supplied). We hope that we can learn from these shortcomings and use the research lessons of the survey to influence the design of any future routine information systems.

The Changing Basis of Assessment

The gradual abandonment, noted in the previous section, of what Cooper [15] has called the 'traditional investigatory, vetting, approval and rejection procedure' owes much to a recognition that foolproof ways of assessing prospective adopters are just not possible. Reviewing the research relating to baby adoption, Triseliotis and Russell conclude:

> 'The attributes that the majority of research studies suggest as being desirable and whose presence among adoptive couples can be predictive of "success" include: being warm and accepting towards the child; a stable marriage and family; acceptance of the adopting role; an accepting attitude towards the family of origin; and helping the adoptee to develop his

emerging personality on the concept of two sets of parents – a biological and a psychological set' [9].

As they are quick to observe, however, to know that these characteristics are important is one thing, but to recognise them in advance is quite another [19]. The task is further complicated by the rapidly changing social context in which assessment decisions are taken. It is not so long ago that religious allegiance, as evidenced by regular attendance at church or chapel, was often considered essential, and agnosticism or atheism could be grounds for rejection [13,20]. Today's requirements for this, as for other aspects of lifestyle, are much less rigid [21]. Indeed, Argent has argued that to expect adoptive parents to remain in stable marriages is itself to expect too much, for we cannot insulate adopting families from the pressures that lead one in three marriages to break up [22]. Perhaps, she concludes,

> 'It is more important to assess whether the partners in a marriage have the strength to become single parents than to try to guarantee that they will stay together.'

Argent has suggested that prospective adopters need 'preparation and support *rather than* assessment and supervision' (emphasis added) but perhaps this is to overstate the change, for some element of assessment is clearly still essential, even if this may increasingly seek to ensure the absence of inappropriate motivations [23,24] rather than the presence of the characteristics of 'the perfect parent'. Just how assessment and preparation should be combined, however, remains problematic, as Triseliotis [25] has observed in describing the use of groups in this field, and there is a continuing need in Strathclyde as elsewhere to be aware of what he has called 'conceptual ambiguities concerning the preparation and selection of carers'.

RESPONDING TO CHILDLESSNESS

In calling for the development of support systems, Argent is representative of a growing trend [26]. This movement predominantly reflects views about the needs of those caring for 'special needs' children, but wider support for baby adopters, and for those considering baby adoption as a result of infertility, is also increasingly being urged. This theme is explored in detail by Brebner and her colleagues in their report of a study of infertile and sub-fertile couples who had gone on to adopt babies [24]. They interviewed the couples shortly after placement and again six months later, assessing how well they had resolved the emotional aspects of their childlessness, and their attitudes to and behaviour with their adopted children. They summarise their findings as follows:

> '... a majority of the infertile parents in the study resolved their disappointment and were able to turn wholeheartedly, with self-confidence and insight, towards adopting a baby as a way of forming a family. However, it was shown that there were a few parents who were still depressed or suffering from low self-esteem, or whose motivation was less than that of the others ... these factors might affect the emotional climate of the home and could have repercussions on the parents' relationship with the adopted child.'

They recommended psychological support for all couples undergoing fertility testing, not only those who may consider adoption, although they emphasise that early support could dissuade couples from deciding to adopt for the wrong reasons. And, while they target these recommendations in the main at the medical profession – urging doctors to recognise both the child-centredness of current adoption practice and the shortage of available babies – there is clearly an emerging role here for social work practitioners working in health care settings.

A social work counselling service for unintentionally childless couples is in fact recommended in the report of a project set up by Dr. Barnardo's [27]. Called 'The Scottish Adoption Advice Service', the project was a telephone counselling scheme with a remit to offer advice on all aspects of adoption. Although greatest use of the service was made by adopted adults, prospective adopters made up the second largest group of enquirers, responsible for almost one-quarter of calls during the period monitored (November 1978 – June 1983). And the great majority of these were from childless couples wishing to adopt a baby; in the words of the report:

> 'The tendency has been for these clients to call the service fairly early on in their dilemma, often within days of having their infertility confirmed by their hospital or G.P.; some even telephoned that same day.'

The report goes on to urge greater recognition of the needs of childless couples, and argues that our response to enquiries from them has focussed too narrowly on the matter of adoption.

AGE OF CHILD FOR WHICH COUPLE WERE APPROVED

While the Barnardo's report stressed that we should not view childless couples merely in terms of their resource-potential, it conceded that a proportion of them could become interested in adopting a 'hard to place' child even though their initial preference was an uncomplicated baby. Indeed, it was critical of the way in which 'agencies usually ask at a very early stage what children a couple will consider', and thereby close down options. The survey touched obliquely on this issue.

One questionnaire item concerned the age of child(ren) for which the Panels considered approved couples suitable. The age-categorisations were based on discussions with adoption advisers, and reflected the kinds of decisions actually taken, and the data were extracted from Adoption Panel minutes. The table below gives the results for all of the approved applicants:

TABLE 3

Age for which approved (percentages)

Division	A	B	C	D	E	TOTAL
Up to 2 years	72	96	71	88	66	78
2–4 years	1.5	–	7	2	5	4
0–4 years	18	2	8	–	16	8
Primary school age	7	1	11	2	6	6
Any age	–	–	1	3	6	2
Not known	1.5	1	2	5	1	2
Total	100	100	100	100	100	100

The region-wide emphasis on baby adoption is clear, and although the age categories make interpretation difficult, variation among the Divisions is once again evident. The concentration on babies is almost total in Division 'B', while 'C' and 'E' are the clearest examples of a more broadly based approach. This pattern is confirmed by figures contained in a report on the Regional Resource Exchange [28], a facility set up to coordinate the needs and resources of the individual Divisions, particularly in relation to 'hard to place' children: Division 'B' referred the fewest foster or adoptive parents. It should be stressed that the figures presented in Table 3 cover the entire period since 1975, and will therefore tend to camouflage the wider recruitment strategy developing during the last few years. Nevertheless, it is evident that there is room for improvement.

CONCLUSION

Geographical variation in adoption practice has often been identified by research studies, and it should not surprise us that an authority as large as Strathclyde has experienced different approaches within its own boundaries. In describing those differences this chapter has tried to point to the important issues which they raise.

Although recent debate has tended to concentrate on 'special needs' children we make no apologies for focussing on baby adoption. The period since our survey was completed has seen an increase locally in the number of very young children available for adoption. This may be a temporary phenomenon but, given Freeman's observation in this volume that significant numbers of young children in temporary foster placements are approaching the point when plans for permanence need to be considered, it may not, and it serves to remind us that adoption practice for *all* children needs to be kept under constant review.

References

1. Tunstill, J. 'Fostering: Direct Work During Placement'. In Lishman, J. (Ed.) *Working with Children. Research Highlights* No.6, University of Aberdeen, 1983, reprint edition Jessica Kingsley, 1987, 123-141.

2. Triseliotis, J. (Ed.) *New Developments in Foster Care and Adoption.* Routledge and Kegan Paul, London, 1980.

3. 'Adoption 1984 – England and Wales' (no author given) *Adoption and Fostering.* 3, 1986, 57-58.

4. Kerr, D. *The Changing Situation: a Statistical View.* Paper given to conference on Child Care Law hosted by ADSW/SCAFA/ SSRG, 28th November, 1987.

5. Report to Strathclyde Regional Council, Social Work Committee, April 1986.

6. Rowe, J. *Yours by Choice.* Routledge and Kegan Paul, London, 1982.

7. McWhinnie, A.M. *Adopted Children: How They Grow Up; A Study of Their Adjustment as Adults.* Routledge and Kegan Paul, London, 1967.

8. Kornitzer, M. *Adoption and Family Life.* Putnam, London, 1968.

9. Triseliotis, J. & Russell, J. *Hard to Place: The Outcome of Adoption and Residential Care.* Heinemann, London, 1984.

10. Barry, N. 'Rejected Adopters Geared for Fight Back' *Social Work Today.* August 25, 1986, 7.

11. Report to Strathclyde Regional Council, Social Work Committee. October 1986.

12. *Room to Grow.* Strathclyde Regional Council, 1979.

13. Goodacre, I. *Adoption Policy and Practice.* Allen and Unwin, London, 1966.

14. *Adoption Policy and Practice Guidelines.* Strathclyde Regional Council, 1980.

15. Cooper, J.D. *Patterns of Family Placement; Current Issues in Fostering and Adoption.* National Children's Bureau, London, 1978.

16. *Fostering Guidelines.* Strathclyde Regional Council, 1985.

17. Triseliotis, J. *Evaluation of Adoption Policy and Practice.* University of Edinburgh Press, Edinburgh, 1970.

18. Jacka, A.A. *Adoption in Brief.* NFER, London, 1973.

19. An investigation of whether psychological tests can help in identifying suitable adopters, which

concluded that they cannot, is reported in Adrian, R.J., Vacchiano, R.B. & Gilbart, T.E. 'Linear Discriminant Function Classification of Accepted and Rejected Adoptive Parents' *Journal of Clinical Psychology*. 2, 1966, 251-254.

20. Pugh, E. *Social Work in Child Care*. Routledge and Kegan Paul, London, 1968.

21. Seed, P. 'Fostering and Adoption as Options for Child Placement – a Discussion of Some Research Conclusions'. In Reinach, E. (Ed.) *Decision Making in Child Care*. Research Highlights No.1, Scottish Academic Press, 1982.

22. Argent, H. 'Opportunities in Adoption' *Adoption and Fostering*. 2, 1985, 17-20.

23. Ripple, L. 'A Follow-up Study of Adopted Children' *Social Service Review*. 4, 1968, 479-499.

24. Brebner, C.M., Sharp, J.D. & Stone, F.H. *The Role of Infertility in Adoption*. British Agencies for Adoption and Fostering, London, 1985.

25. Triseliotis, J. 'The Preparation and Selection of Adoptive and Foster Parents'. In Triseliotis, J. (Ed.) *Groupwork in Adoptive and Foster Care*. Batsford, London. Forthcoming (1988).

26. For example, O'Hara, G. 'Developing Post-placement Services in Lothian' *Adoption and Fostering*. 4, 1986, 38-42.

27. Lindsay, M. & McGarry, K. *Adoption Counselling – A Talking Point*. Dr. Barnardo's, Scottish Division, 1984.

28. *Policy and Procedures for the Regional Resource Exchange*. Strathclyde Regional Council, Social Work Department, 1980.

Research Highlights in Social Work

This topical series of books examines areas currently of particular interest to those in social and community work and related fields. Each book draws together a collection of articles on different aspects of the subject under discussion – highlighting relevant research and drawing out implications for policy and practice.

The books are concise yet comprehensive, providing policy-makers, practitioners, researchers and managers with a readable and useful source of information.

The project is under the general direction of Professor Gerard Rochford.